PIANO ACCOMPANIMENTS 4

TEACHER'S EDITION

SHARE the MUSIC
MACMILLAN/McGRAW-HILL

SERIES AUTHORS

Judy Bond
Coordinating Author

René Boyer-Alexander

Margaret Campbelle-Holman

Marilyn Copeland Davidson
Coordinating Author

Robert de Frece

Mary Goetze
Coordinating Author

Doug Goodkin

Betsy M. Henderson

Michael Jothen

Carol King

Vincent P. Lawrence
Coordinating Author

Nancy L.T. Miller

Ivy Rawlins

Susan Snyder
Coordinating Author

The page number below the song title indicates the corresponding page in the pupil's editions for Grades 2–6 and in the Teacher's Editions for all grades. The symbol ▼ has been added to some of the piano accompaniments to indicate the line breaks in the pupil's edition. For example, $\frac{2}{▼}$ indicates the beginning of the second line of music in the pupil's edition.

Some songs in the **Share the Music** program are not represented in this **Piano Accompaniments** book as they may not be appropriate for accompaniment on the piano. It may be more appropriate when teaching these songs to have them performed a cappella or with unpitched percussion instruments or body percussion.

Acknowledgments for **Piano Accompaniments** can be found at the back of this book.

Cover Design: Robert Brook Allen, A Boy and His Dog
Cover Photography: McGraw-Hill School Division

Published by Macmillan/McGraw-Hill, of McGraw-Hill Education, a division of The McGraw-Hill Companies, Inc., Two Penn Plaza, New York, New York 10121.

Copyright © 2003, 2000 by Macmillan/McGraw-Hill. All rights reserved. No part of this publication may be reproduced or distributed in any form or by any means, or stored in a database or retrieval system, without the prior written consent of The McGraw-Hill Companies, Inc., including, but not limited to, network storage or transmission, or broadcast for distance learning.

Printed in the United States of America

ISBN 0-02-295583-6 / 4

1 2 3 4 5 6 7 8 9 066 07 06 05 04 03 02

TABLE OF CONTENTS

Piano Accompaniments are in the order of song appearance in the Pupil's Edition and Teacher's Editions.

TIME FOR SINGING!
Don't Let the Music Stop 2
Oh, Won't You Sit Down? 7
Let Music Surround You 9
Somos el barco (We Are the Boat) 10
The Wabash Cannonball 14
This Is My Country 16

UNIT 1
Sir Duke 18
Take Me Home, Country Roads .. 22
I Let Her Go, Go 27
'Way Down Yonder in the Brickyard. 29
Mongolian Night Song 32
Hi! Ho! The Rattlin' Bog 35
Fed My Horse 37
The California Song 38

UNIT 2
City of New Orleans 41
Trail to Mexico 48
Four White Horses 50
The Old Carrion Crow 52
En la feria de San Juan
  (In the Market of San Juan) 55
Down the Road 57
Swapping Song 60
When I Was a Lad 62
Orchestra Song 67
Encore: Singin' in the Rain 70

UNIT 3
Oh, Susanna 72
I Don't Care If the Rain
  Comes Down 74
La pájara pinta
  (The Speckled Bird) 76
Pay Me My Money Down 79
One More River 81
Come and Sing Together 84
The Eagle 87
I's the B'y 90
When I First Came to This Land . 92
Over the Sea to Skye 94

UNIT 4
It's a Lovely Day Today 96
Tina Singu 100
Hosanna, Me Build a House 103
Sarasponda 108
Little David, Play on Your Harp .. 109
Hoe Ana Te Vaka
  (Paddle the Canoe) 110
Sourwood Mountain 114
A Tragic Story 116
Encore: Hambone 118

UNIT 5
The Song of the World's
  Last Whale 120
Take Time in Life 123
Calypso 125

Tum-Balalaika 129
Hei Tama Tu Tama 131
Aquaqua 132
Wade in the Water 133
Music Alone Shall Live
  (Himmel und Erde) 136
Waltzing with Bears 138
Las mañanitas
  (The Morning Song) 143
Push the Business On 144

UNIT 6
Comes Once in a Lifetime 146
I Can Be 149
This Pretty Planet 156
The Cat Came Back 158
Old Joe Clark 162
The Court of King Carraticus ... 164
Michie Banjo 166
Simple Gifts 168
Garden Song 170
Donna, Donna 172

CELEBRATIONS
The Star-Spangled Banner 175
America, the Beautiful 178
Sing a Song of Peace 180
America 182
The Boogie Woogie Ghost 183
The Ghost of John 187
Dry Bones 188
For Health and Strength 192
A Mince Pie or Pudding 193
Bonhomme! Bonhomme! 194
Winter Fantasy 197
In the Window 202
Para pedir posada 204
Entren santos peregrinos
  (Enter, Holy Pilgrims) 208
Dale, dale, dale! 209
A Holly Jolly Christmas 211
O Tannenbaum!
  (O, Christmas Tree!) 214
Somewhere in My Memory ... 215
Dormi, dormi (Sleep, Sleep) ... 217
We Three Kings 220
The Twelve Days of Christmas .. 222
Suk san wan pi mai
  (New Year's Song) 228
Martin's Cry 230
Down by the Riverside 234
Macnamara's Band 238
Tree Song 242

MUSIC LIBRARY
More Songs to Read
I Love the Mountains 246
Night Song 248
Go 'Round the Mountain 249
Babylon's Fallin' 250
Page's Train 251

I Am a Cat 252
Lady, Come Down and See ... 253
Dinah 254
Ida Red 255
The Old Chisholm Trail 257
Old Tar River 258
Heave-Ho Me Laddies 260
My Horses Ain't Hungry 262
The Derby Ram 263
Lots o' Fish in Bonavist' Harbor . 266
Old Dan Tucker 268
My Dame Hath a Lame,
  Tame Crane 270
To Stop the Train 271
Before Dinner 272
Hop Up and Jump Up 273
Oliver Cromwell 275
Who's Got a Fishpole? 277
The Boll Weevil 278
Alleluia, Amen 281
San lun tsa (Three-Wheeled
  Taxi) 282
John Kanaka 283
Ah, Poor Bird 285
Chickalileeo 286
Artsa Alinu (Our Land) 288
Korobushka 289
O musique 291
Alouette 292

Choral Anthology
The Path to the Moon 293
Wind on the Hill 298
Haida 300
And Where Is Home? 302
Don't Let the Music Stop 307

Musical
The Golden Goose
Happiness 310
No Matter What 317
Things That Grow 322
Barter Song 326
Bird in the Water 330
Stone Pounding 336

HAL LEONARD SHOWSTOPPERS
Land of a Thousand Dances
At the Hop 338
Dancing in the Street 343
We Got the Beat 348
The Loco-Motion 353
Bristol Stomp 358
Down at the Twist and Shout ... 364
Twist and Shout 369
Land of a Thousand Dances ... 374

Acknowledgments 381
Alphabetical Song Index 384

Don't Let the Music Stop I

PUPIL'S PAGE viii

Words and Music by Eugene Butler
Piano Accompaniment by Linda Worsley

Oh, Won't You Sit Down?

PUPIL'S PAGE 2

African American Spiritual

Let Music Surround You

PUPIL'S PAGE 3

Words and Music by Fran Addicott
Piano Accompaniment by Carol Jay

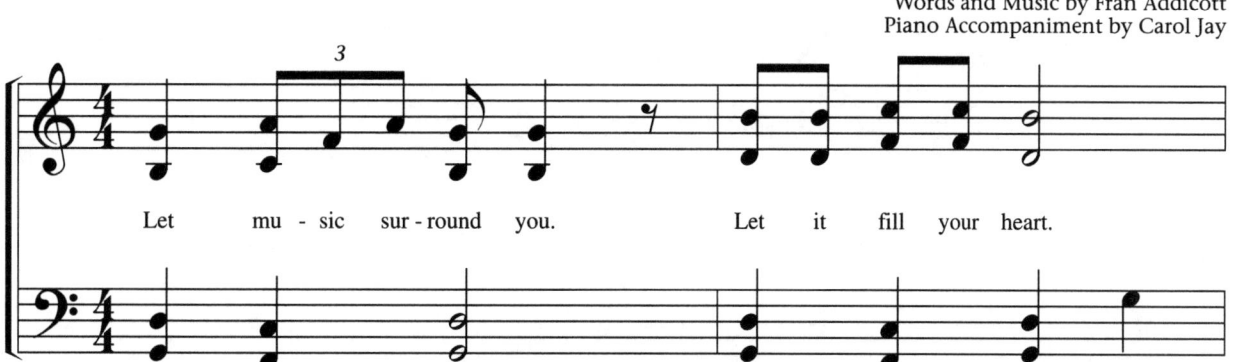

Let mu - sic sur - round you. Let it fill your heart.

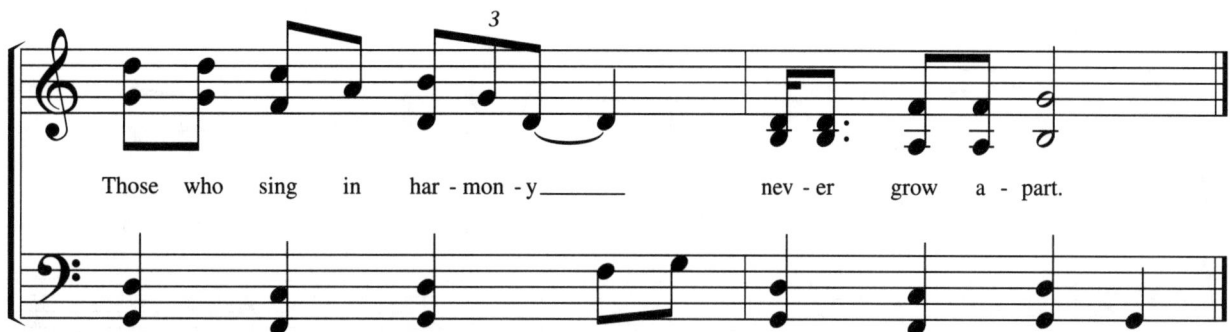

Those who sing in har - mon - y _____ nev - er grow a - part.

Somos el barco
We Are the Boat

PUPIL'S PAGE 4

Words and Music by Lorre Wyatt
Piano Accompaniment by Warren Stine

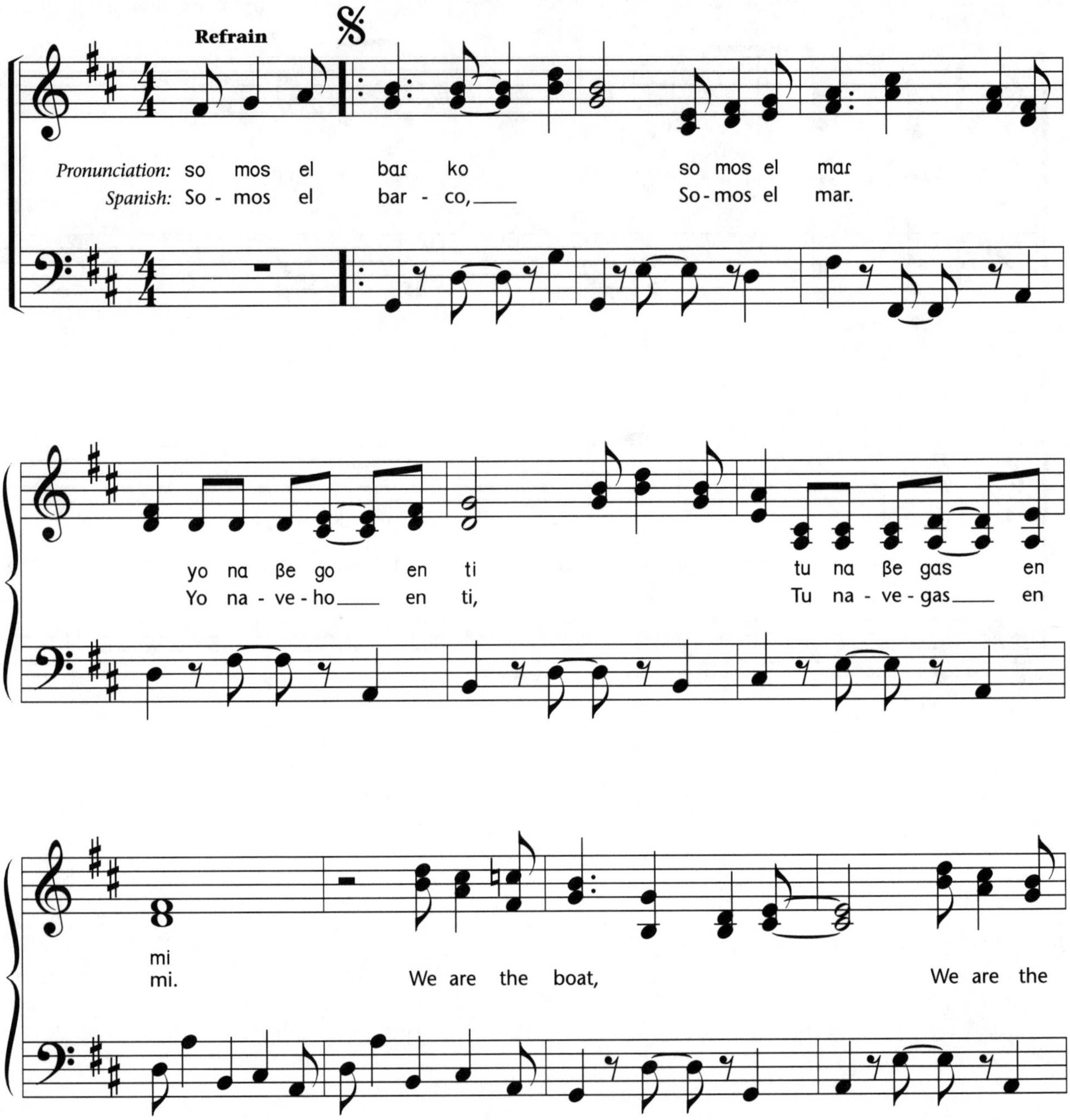

Pronunciation: so mos el bar ko　　so mos el mar　　yo na βe go en ti　　tu na βe gas en　　mi.
Spanish: So-mos el bar-co,　　So-mos el mar.　　Yo na-ve-ho en ti,　　Tu na-ve-gas en　　mi.

We are the boat,　　We are the

The Wabash Cannonball

PUPIL'S PAGE 6

Words and Music by William Kindt
Piano Arrangement by Steve Hoover

2. Now she came in from Birmingham on a cold and frosty day,
   As she rolled into the station you could hear the people say,
   "There's a gal out there from Tennessee, she's long, boy, and tall,
   She's the modern combination called the Wabash Cannonball."
   Refrain

3. Now the Eastern states are dandy, so all the people say,
   From New York to Saint Louis and Chicago by the way,
   From the lakes of Minnesota where the rippling waters fall,
   No change in standard gauging on the Wabash Cannonball.
   Refrain

This Is My Country

PUPIL'S PAGE 7

Music by Al Jacobs
Words by Don Raye

16

Sir Duke

PUPIL'S PAGE 10

Words and Music by Stevie Wonder
Piano Accompaniment by Carol Jay

Take Me Home, Country Roads

PUPIL'S PAGE 12

Words and Music by Bill Danoffk,
Taffy Nivert, and John Denver
Piano Accompaniment by Carol Jay

22

I Let Her Go, Go

PUPIL'S PAGE 15

Folk Song from Trinidad and Tobago
Adapted by Carol King
Piano Accompaniment by Carol Jay

Instrumental not in Pupil's Edition

28

'Way Down Yonder in the Brickyard

PUPIL'S PAGE 17

Traditional African American Game Song
As performed by the Georgia Sea Island Singers
Piano Accompaniment by Carol Jay

Mongolian Night Song

PUPIL'S PAGE 19

Traditional Inner Mongolian Song
Collected and Translated by Gloria Kiester
Piano Accompaniment by Bill and Pat Medley

1. Lit-tle girl who tends the sheep, Brings them to the fold to sleep.
2. In the moon-light's gold-en glow, Soft the wind be-gins to blow.

Lit-tle lambs are bounc-ing by to their moth-er's bleat-ing cry,
Lit-tle lambs are fast a-sleep, ly-ing by the oth-er sheep.

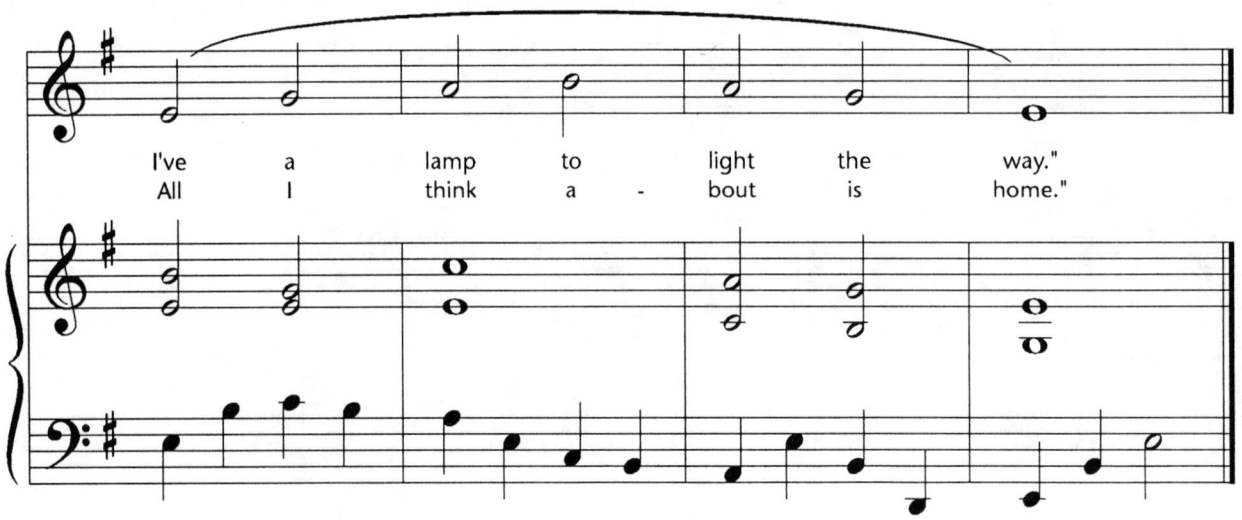

Hi! Ho! The Rattlin' Bog

PUPIL'S PAGE 23

Irish Folk Song
Piano Accompaniment by Anna Marie Spallina

35

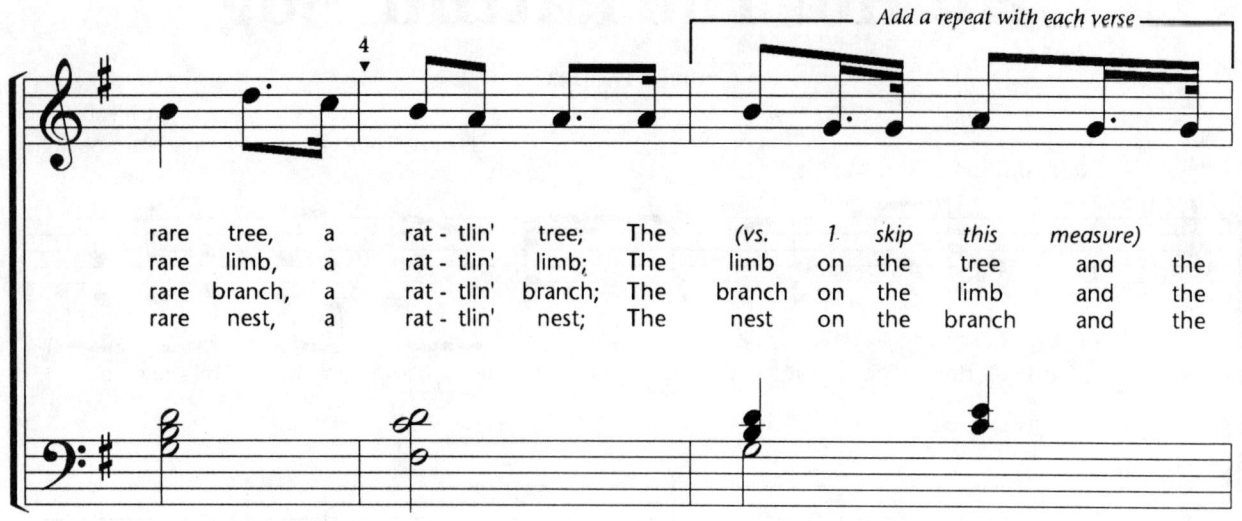

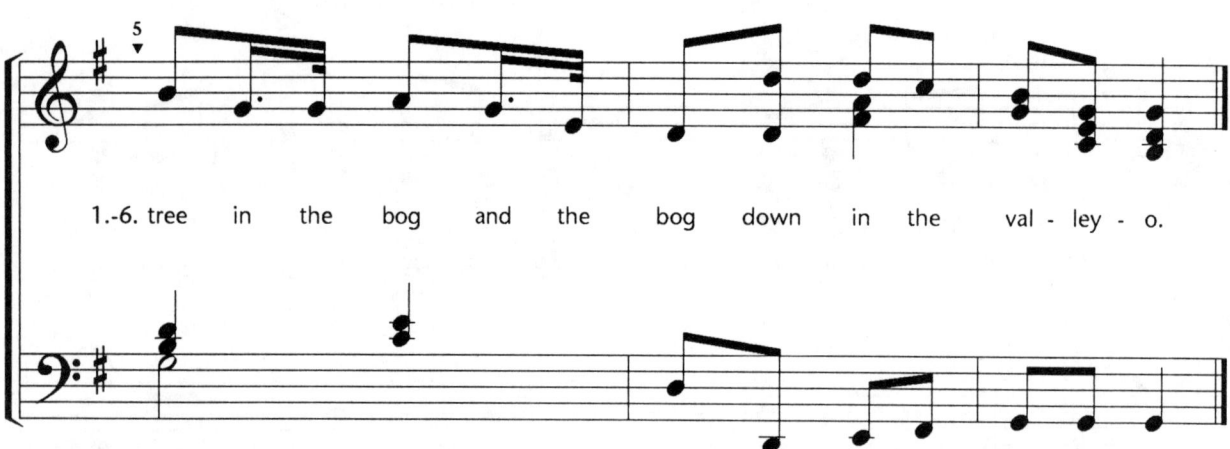

5. Now in this nest there was an egg, a rare egg,
   a rattlin' egg;
   The egg in the nest and the. . . .

6. Now in this egg there was a bird, a rare bird,
   a rattlin' bird;
   The bird in the egg and the. . . .

Fed My Horse

PUPIL'S PAGE 31

Southern Appalachian Folk Song
Piano Accompaniment by Carol Jay

Fed my horse in a pop-lar trough, Fed my horse in a pop-lar trough,

Fed my horse in a pop-lar trough, Then she caught the whoop-ing cough.

Coy ma-lin-do Kill-ko, kill-ko; Coy ma-lin-do Kill-ko me.

The California Song

PUPIL'S PAGE 48

American Folk Song
Piano Accompaniment by Anna Marie Spallina

1. We've formed our band and we are all well manned To journey afar to the promised land, Where the golden ore is
2. Oh, the gold in thar most any-whar, They dig it out with an iron bar, And where it's thick with a
3. Oh don't you cry or heave a sigh, For we'll come back again bye and bye, Don't have fear or
4. We expect our share of the coarsest fare, And sometimes sleep in the open air, Upon the cold ground we will

City of New Orleans

PUPIL'S PAGE 56

Words and Music by Steve Goodman
Piano Accompaniment by Steve Hoover

41

45

2. Night time on the City of New Orleans,
   Changin' cars in Memphis, Tennessee.
   Halfway home, we'll be there by mornin'
   through the Mississippi darkness rollin' down to the sea.
   But all the towns and people seem to fade into a bad dream
   and the steel rail still ain't heard the news.
   The conductor sings his songs again
   the passengers will please refrain
   this train's got the disappearin' railroad blues.
   Good night America, how are you?
   Say don't you know me, I'm your native son.
   I'm the train they call the City of New Orleans.
   I'll be gone five hundred miles when the day is done.

Trail to Mexico

PUPIL'S PAGES 59, 74

American Cowboy Song
Music Adapted by Carol King
Piano Accompaniment by Anna Marie Spallina

1. I made my up mind in the ear-ly morn To leave the home where I was born, To leave my
2. 'Twas in the year of eight-y-three That A. J. Stin - son hired me. He said, "Young
3. 'Twas in the spring-time of the year I vol-un-teered to drive the steers. I'll tell you,

Vocal ostinato
Rid-in' on the West-ern Trail. Up in the sad-dle all day.

48

Four White Horses

PUPIL'S PAGE 60

Caribbean Folk Song
Collected by Lois Choksy
Piano Accompaniment by Carol Jay

The Old Carrion Crow

PUPIL'S PAGE 62

Nova Scotian Folk Song
Piano Accompaniment by Mary Goetze

4. The old sow died and the bells did toll,
   Fol the riddle, all the riddle hey ding doh,
   And the little pigs cried and prayed for her soul.
   Refrain
5. Oh, now the old sow's dead and gone,
   Fol the riddle, all the riddle hey ding doh,
   And the little pigs play and waddle on,
   Refrain

En la feria de San Juan
In the Market of San Juan

Puerto Rican Folk Song
Piano Accompaniment by Kay Evans

PUPIL'S PAGE 66

2. En la feria de San Juan
yo compré un tambor.
Ton, ton, ton, el tambor, . . .

In the market of San Juan
I bought myself a drum.
Tum, tum, tum, tum, the drum.

3. yo compré una guitarra,
tara, tara, tara, la guitarra, . . .

I bought a guitar,
tara, tara, tara, the guitar.

4. yo compré un violín,
Lin, lin, lin el violin, . . .

I bought a violin,
Lin, lin, lin, the violin.

Down the Road

PUPIL'S PAGE 76

American Folk Song
Piano Accompaniment by Carol Jay

Swapping Song

PUPIL'S PAGE 82

Appalachian Folk Song
Piano Accompaniment by Carol Jay

1. When I was a little boy I lived by myself; All the bread and cheese I had, I put it on the shelf.
2. Rats and the mice, they led me such a life, I had to go to London to get myself a wife.
3. Roads were so long and the lanes were so narrow, I had to bring her home in an old wheelbarrow.
4. Wheelbarrow broke and my wife got a fall; Down came the wheelbarrow, wife and all.

5. Swapped my wheelbarrow and got me a horse;
   Then I rode from cross to cross.

6. Swapped my horse and got me a mare;
   Then I rode from fair to fair.

7. Swapped my mare and got me a mule;
   Then I rode like a doggone fool.

8. Swapped my mule and got me a goat;
   When I got on him, he wouldn't tote.

9. Swapped my goat and got me a sheep;
   Then I rode myself to sleep.

10. Swapped my sheep and got me a cow;
    And in that trade I just learned how.

11. Swapped my cow and got me a calf;
    In that trade I just lost half.

12. Swapped my calf and got me a hen;
    Oh what a pretty thing I had then.

13. Swapped my hen and got me a rat;
    Put it on the haystack away from the cat.

14. Swapped my rat and got me a mouse;
    Its tail caught afire and burned up my house.

When I Was a Lad

PUPIL'S PAGE 96

Music by Arthur S. Sullivan
Words by William S. Gilbert
Piano Accompaniment by Carol Jay

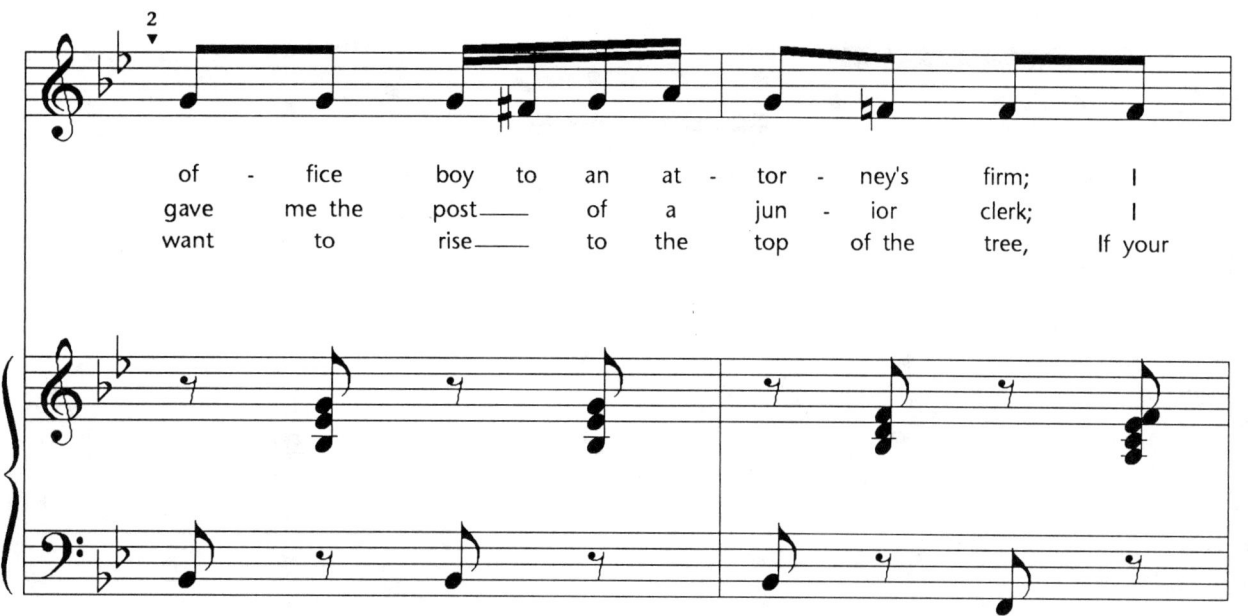

Orchestra Song

PUPIL'S PAGE 98

Austrian Round
Piano Accompaniment by Carol Jay

Singin' in the Rain

PUPIL'S PAGE 100

Music by Nacio Herb Brown
Words by Arthur Freed
Piano Accompaniment by Bill and Pat Medley

70

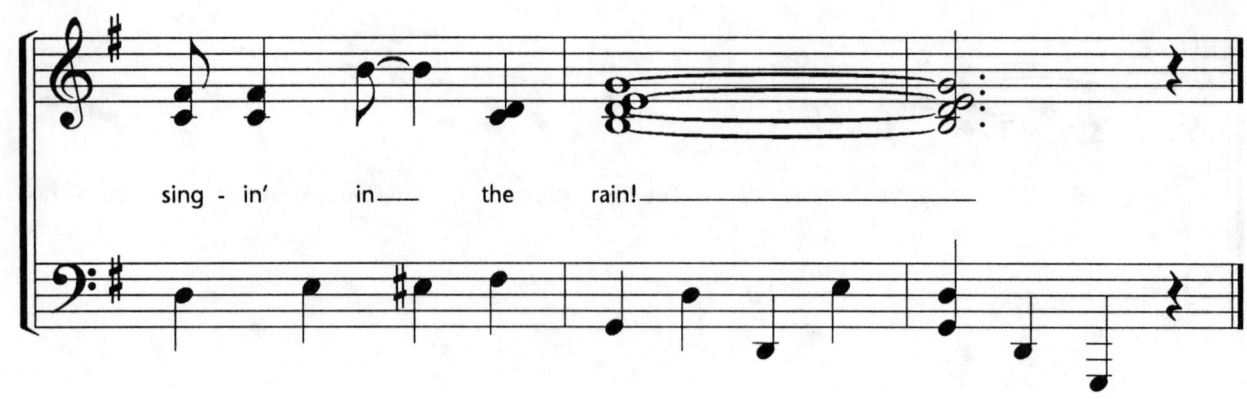

Oh, Susanna

PUPIL'S PAGE 107

Words and Music by Stephen Foster
Piano Accompaniment by Bill and Pat Medley

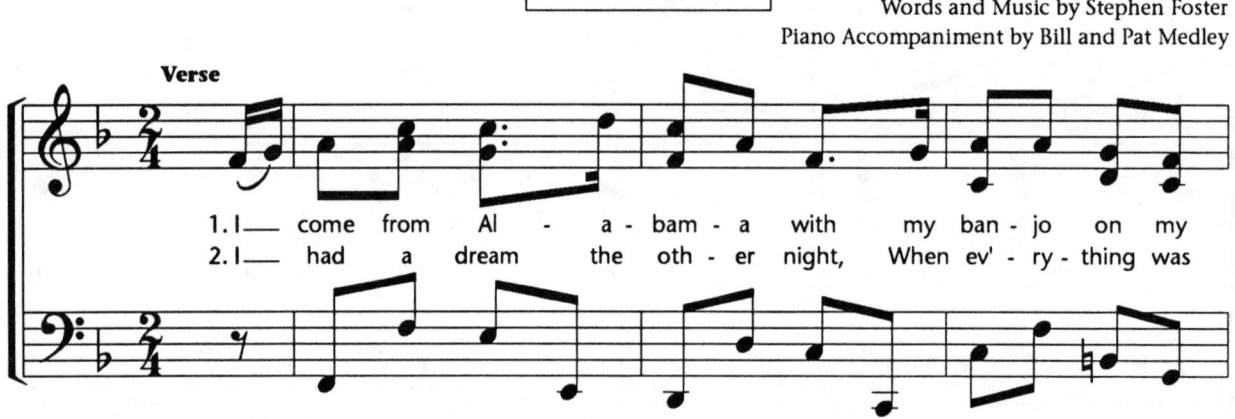

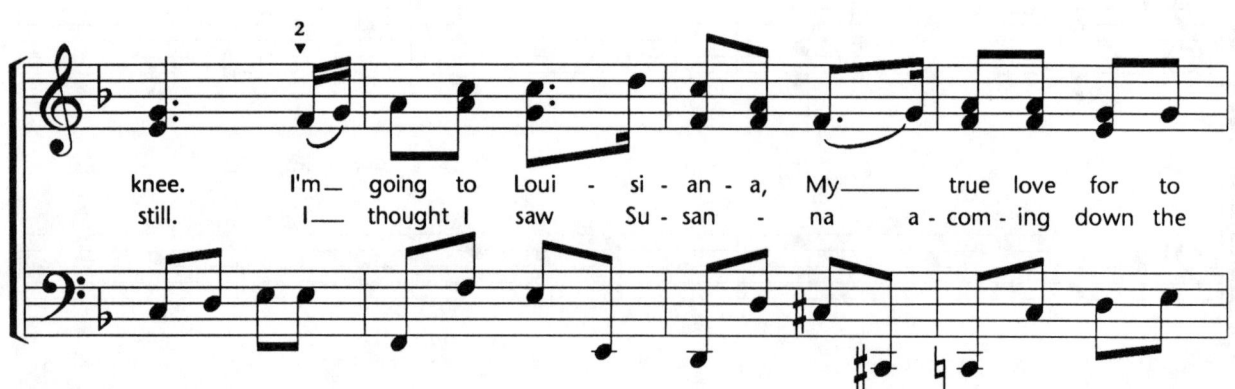

I Don't Care If the Rain Comes Down

PUPIL'S PAGE 108

American Folk Song
Piano Accompaniment by Carol Jay

74

La pájara pinta
The Speckled Bird

Mexican Folk Song
Piano Accompaniment by Carol Jay

Pay Me My Money Down

PUPIL'S PAGE 111

African American Work Song from
The Georgia Sea Islands
Collected and Adapted by Lydia A. Parrish
Piano Accompaniment by William N. Simon

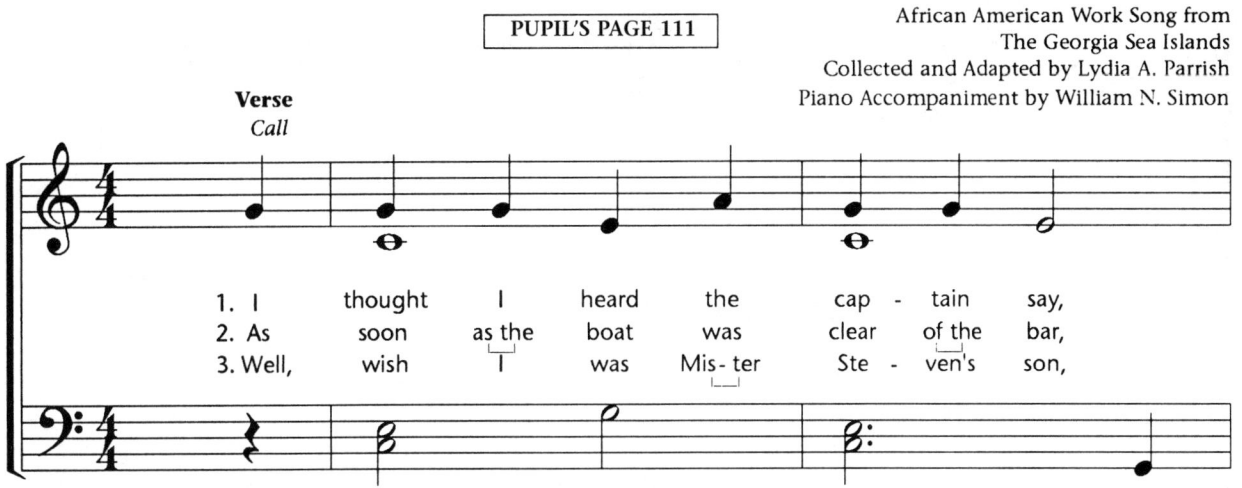

1. I thought I heard the cap-tain say,
2. As soon as the boat was clear of the bar,
3. Well, wish I was Mis-ter Ste-ven's son,

"Pay me my mon-ey down,"—
To-mor-row is our
He knocked me down with the
Sit on the bank and

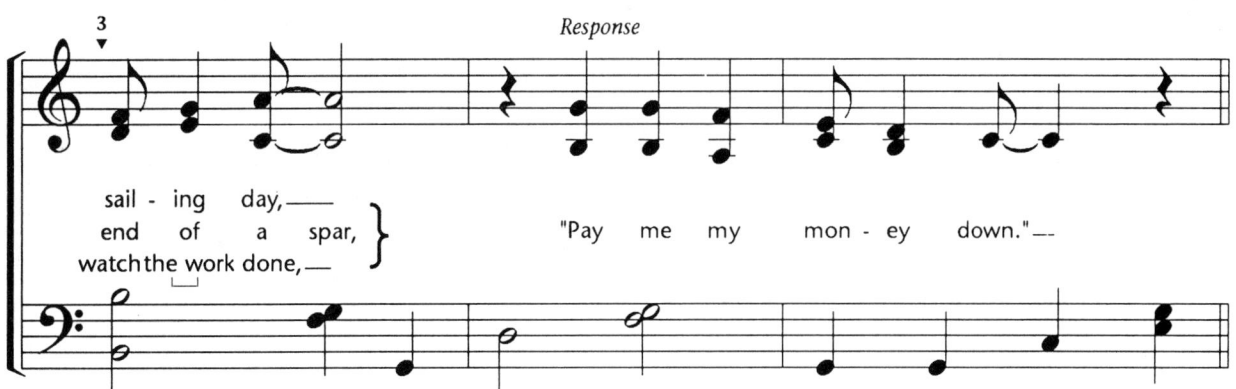

sail-ing day,—
end of a spar,
watch the work done,—
"Pay me my mon-ey down."—

PAY ME MY MONEY DOWN. Words and Music by Lydia A. Parrish.
TRO- Copyright 1942 (renewed) Hollis Music, Inc., New York, NY. Used by permission.

One More River

PUPIL'S PAGE 112

Nineteenth Century College Song
Piano Accompaniment by Carol Jay

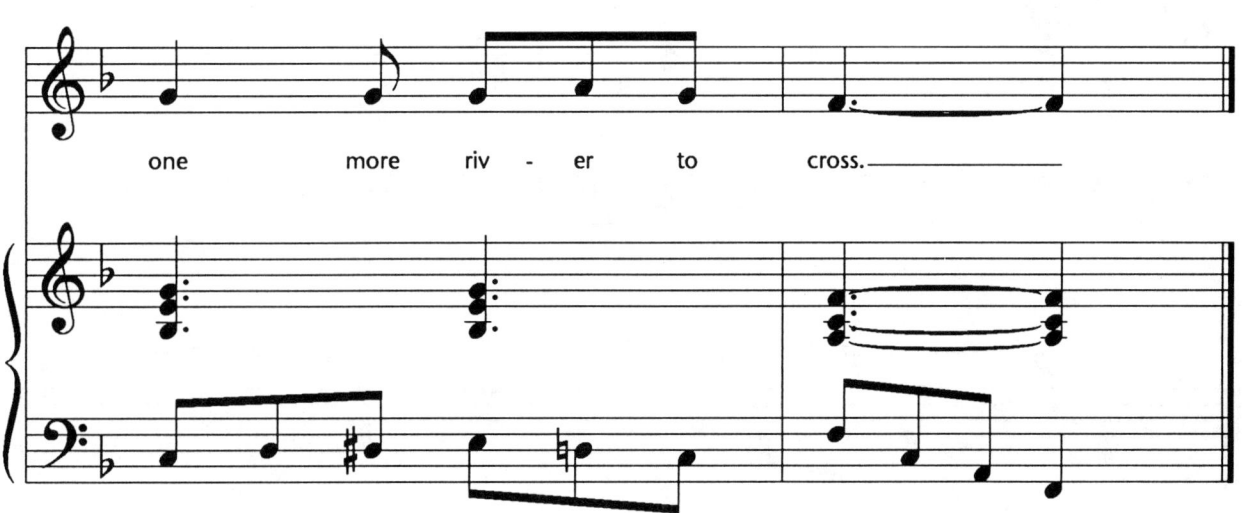

4. The animals went in three by three; . . .
   The bear, the bug, and the bumblebee; . . .
Refrain

5. The animals went in four by four; . . .
   The hippopotamus stuck in the door; . . .
Refrain

6. The animals went in five by five; . . .
   "It's raining," said Noah, "so look alive!" . . .
Refrain

7. The animals went in six by six; . . .
   The monkeys were up to monkey tricks; . . .
Refrain

8. The animals went in sev'n by sev'n; . . .
   The rabbit said, "I wish I had driv'n." . . .
Refrain

9. The animals went in eight by eight; . . .
   "That's 'nuff," said Noah, and slammed the gate! . . .
Refrain

10. And as they talked of this and that; . . .
    The ark, it bumped on Ararat; . . .
Refrain

Come and Sing Together

PUPIL'S PAGES 115, 138

Traditional Hungarian Melody
Piano Accompaniment by Carol Jay

©1990 *Canons, Songs and Blessings: A Kemp Family Collection*
(CGC-27) By Helm and John Kemp, Choristers Guild

The Eagle

PUPIL'S PAGE 118

Music by Hap Palmer
Words by Martha Cheney
Piano Accompaniment by Lynn Freeman Olson

1. Born for a west-ern sky, sweep-ing a cir-cle as he flies.
2. Brave and a hun-ter's son, the land was his 'til he met a gun. } He was free
3. There on a moun-tain high, wound-ed ea-gle wants to die.

mf 4. Dreaming of days gone by,
when little children watched him fly. . . .

I's the B'y

PUPIL'S PAGE 132

Newfoundland Folk Song
Piano Accompaniment by Bill and Pat Medley

1. I's the b'y that builds the boat, And, I's the b'y that sails her! I's the b'y that catches the fish, And
2. Sods and rinds to cov-er you flake, Cakes and tea for sup-per, Cod-fish in the spring o' the year,
3. I don't want your mag-got-y fish, That's no good for win-ter, I could buy as good as that

When I First Came to This Land

4. . . . Then I got myself a wife. . . .
called my wife *Joy-of-my-life.*

5. . . .Then I got myself a son. . .
told my son My work's done.

Over the Sea to Skye

PUPIL'S PAGE 149

Music by Annie MacLeod
Words by Sir Harold Boulton
Piano Accompaniment by William N. Simon

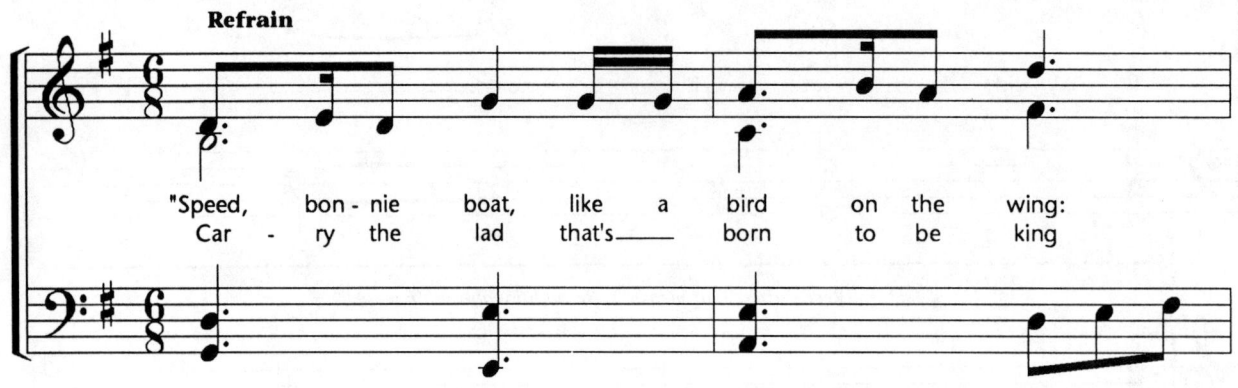

4. Burned are our homes, exile and death
   Scatter the loyal men;
   Yet ere the sword cool in the sheath,
   Charlie will come again.

It's a Lovely Day Today

PUPIL'S PAGE 156

Words and Music by Irving Berlin
Piano Accompaniment by Linda Worsley

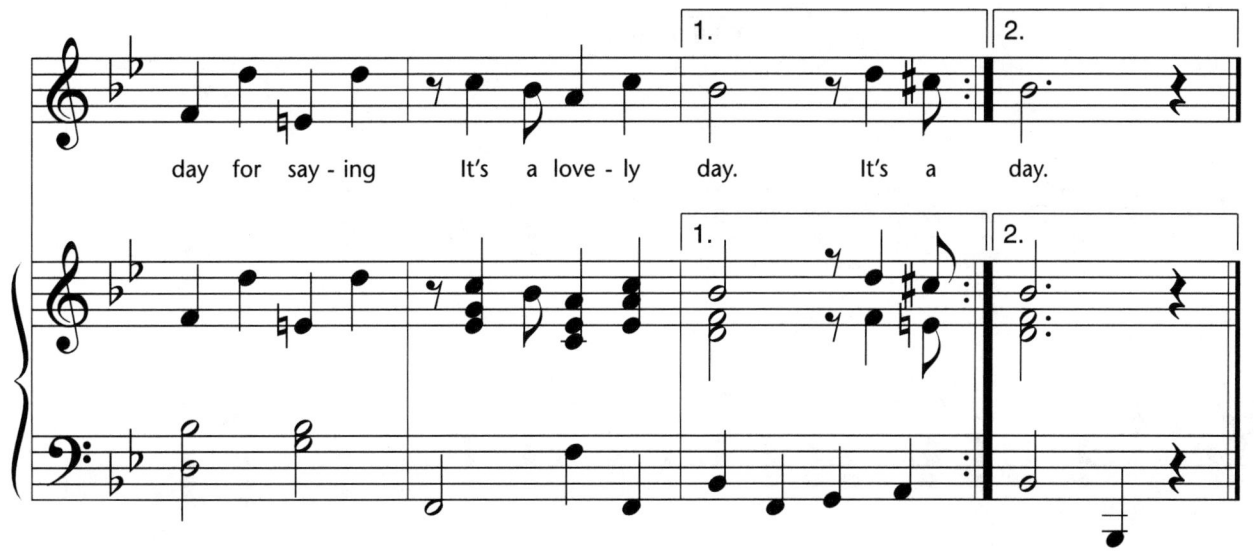

Tina Singu

PUPIL'S PAGE 158

Song from Lesotho
As Sung by Kathleen Hill
Piano Accompaniment by Carol Jay

100

Hosanna, Me Build a House

PUPIL'S PAGE 164

Jamaican Calypso
Piano Accompaniment by Carol Jay

Sarasponda

PUPIL'S PAGE 167

Dutch Spinning Song

Little David, Play on Your Harp

PUPIL'S PAGE 168

African American Spiritual
Piano Accompaniment by MMH

Hoe Ana Te Vaka
Paddle the Canoe

Tahitian Folk Song
Collected and Transcribed by Kathy Sorensen
Piano Accompaniment by Carol Jay

PUPIL'S PAGE 181

Sourwood Mountain

PUPIL'S PAGE 196

Appalachian Folk Song

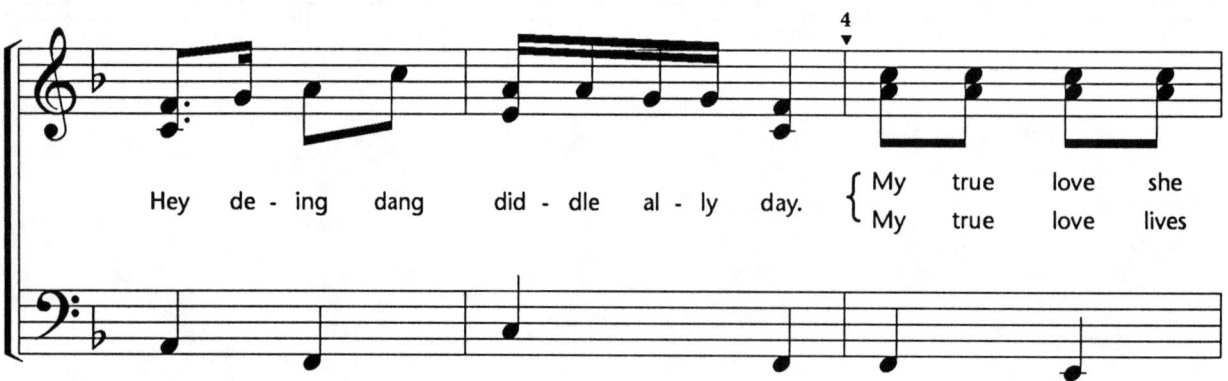

A Tragic Story

PUPIL'S PAGE 197

Music by Benjamin Britten
Words by William M. Thackeray
Piano Accompaniment by Carol Jay

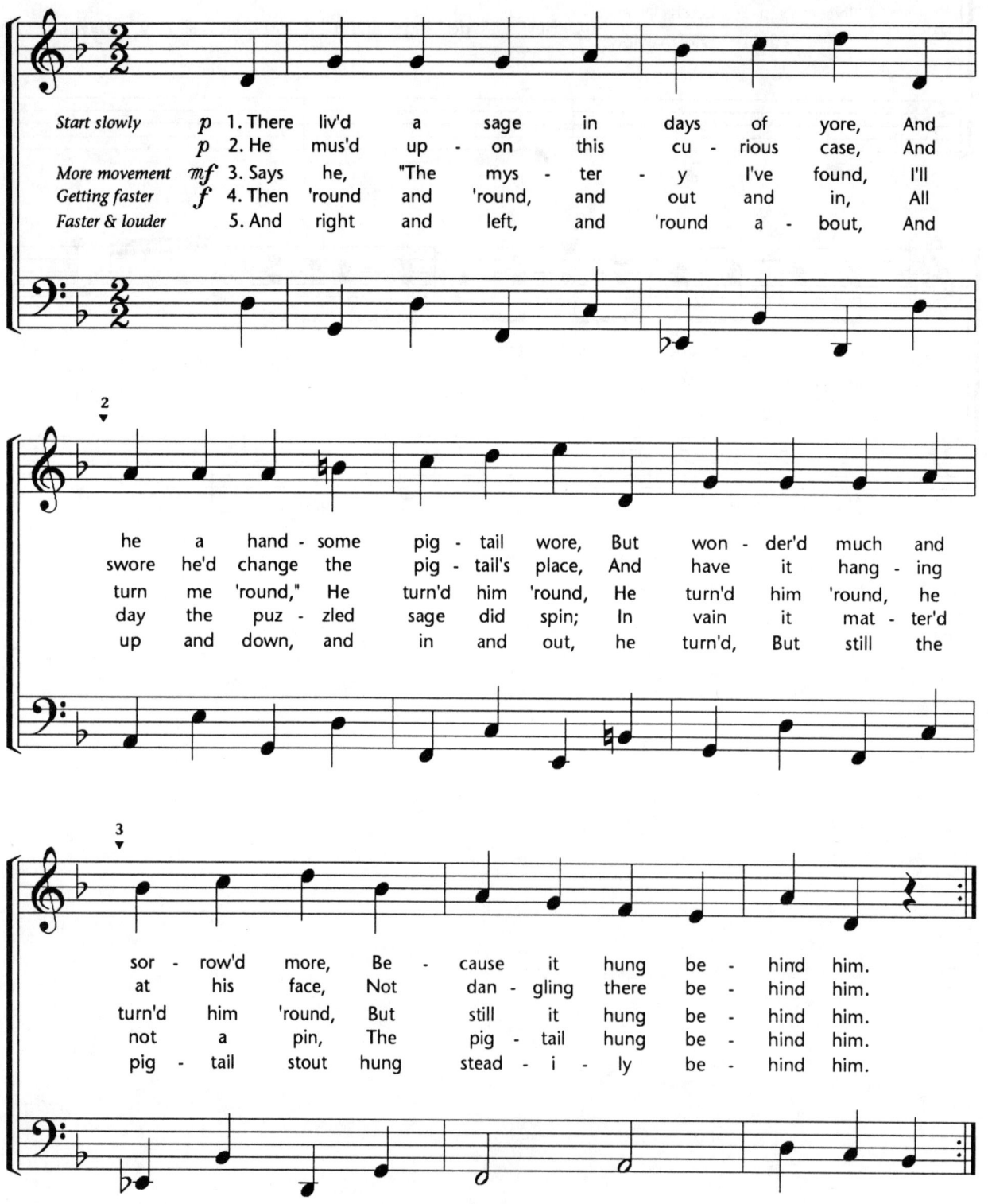

Hambone

PUPIL'S PAGE 200

African American Hand Jive Game
Piano Accompaniment by Carol Jay

1. Ham - bone, Ham - bone, have you heard?
2. If that mock - in' - bird don't sing,
3. If that dia - mond ring turns brass,

Pop - pa's gon - na buy me a mock - in' - bird.
Pop - pa's gon - na buy me a dia - mond ring.
Pop - pa's gon - na buy me a look - ing glass.

4. If that looking glass gets broke,
   Poppa's gonna buy me a billy goat.

5. Hambone, Hambone where you been?
   "Round the world and back again."

6. Hambone, Hambone, where's your wife?
   "She's in the kitchen eatin' rice."

The Song of the World's Last Whale

PUPIL'S PAGE 205

Words and Music by Peter Seeger
Piano Accompaniment by Carol Jay

4. Down in the Antarctic the harpoons wait,
   But it's upon the land they decide my fate.
   In London Town they'll be telling the tale,
   If it's life or death for the world's last whale.

5. So here's a little test to see how you feel,
   Here's a little test for this age of the automobile.
   If we can save our singers in the sea,
   Perhaps there's a chance to save you and me.

Take Time in Life

PUPIL'S PAGE 206

Liberian Folk Song
Piano Accompaniment by Carol Jay

123

Calypso

PUPIL'S PAGE 208

Words and Music by John Denver
Piano Accompaniment by Bill and Pat Medley

Tum-Balalaika

PUPIL'S PAGE 210

Russian Yiddish Folk Song
Piano Accompaniment by Carol Jay

129

Hei Tama Tu Tama

PUPIL'S PAGE 212

Traditional Maori Children's Counting Game
Piano Accompaniment by Carol Jay

Tahi, rua, toru are the words for "one, two, three." *Whitu, waru, iwa* are "seven, eight, nine."
Wha, rima, ono are "four, five, six." *Tekau* is "ten" and *tama* means "young boy."

Aquaqua

PUPIL'S PAGE 219

Israeli Children's Game
Collected by Rita Klinger
Piano Accompaniment by Carol Jay

Nonsense: A - qua qua del - la o - mar qua qua qua del si - ma tri - co tri - co tra va - lo va - lo va - lo va - lo va - lo va - lo va - lo 1 2 3 4 5

Wade in the Water

PUPIL'S PAGES 229, 236

African American Spiritual
Piano Accompaniment by Carol Jay

133

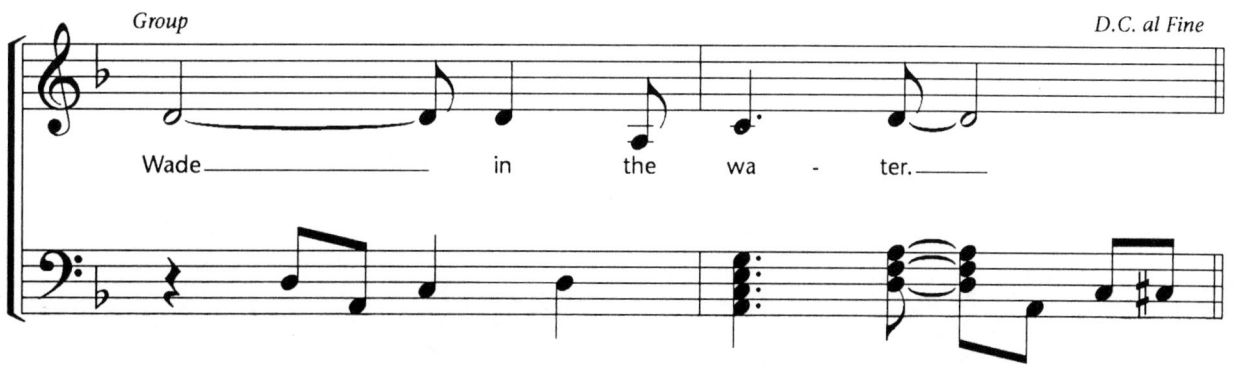

*Note: Cue notes may be sung or replaced with improvisation.

Music Alone Shall Live
Himmel und Erde

PUPIL'S PAGE 231

German Round
Words Adapted by MMH
Piano Accompaniment by Carol Jay

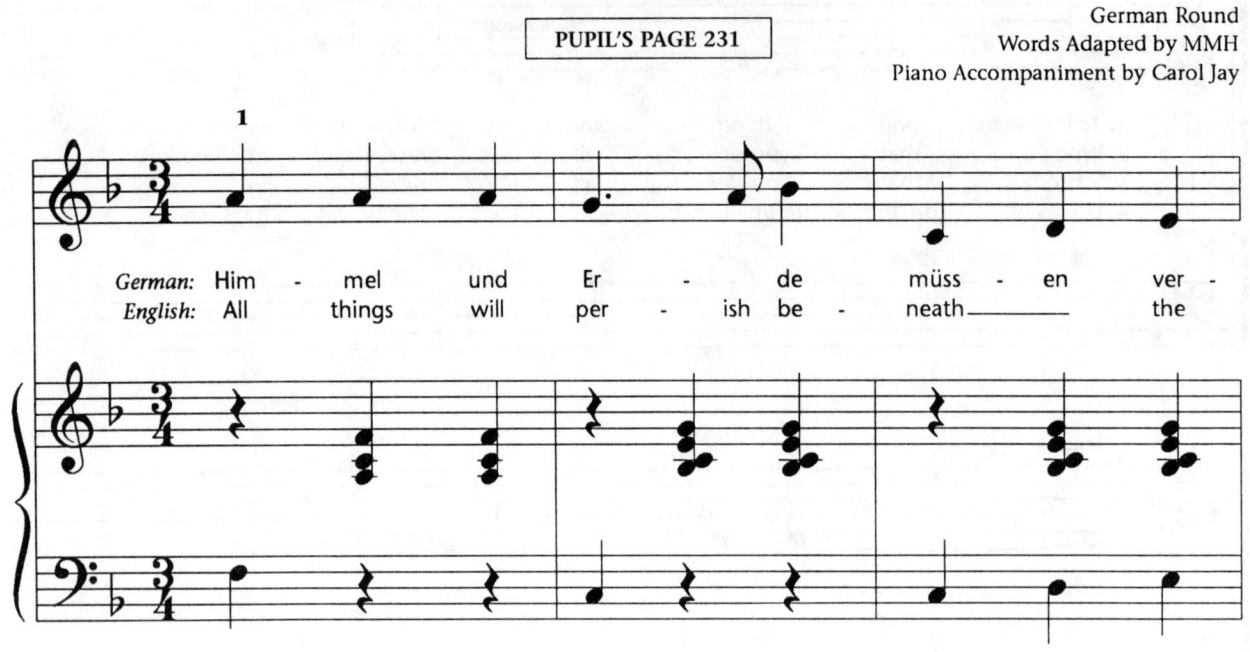

Waltzing with Bears

PUPIL'S PAGE 242

Words and Music by Dale Marxen
Piano Accompaniment by Carol Jay

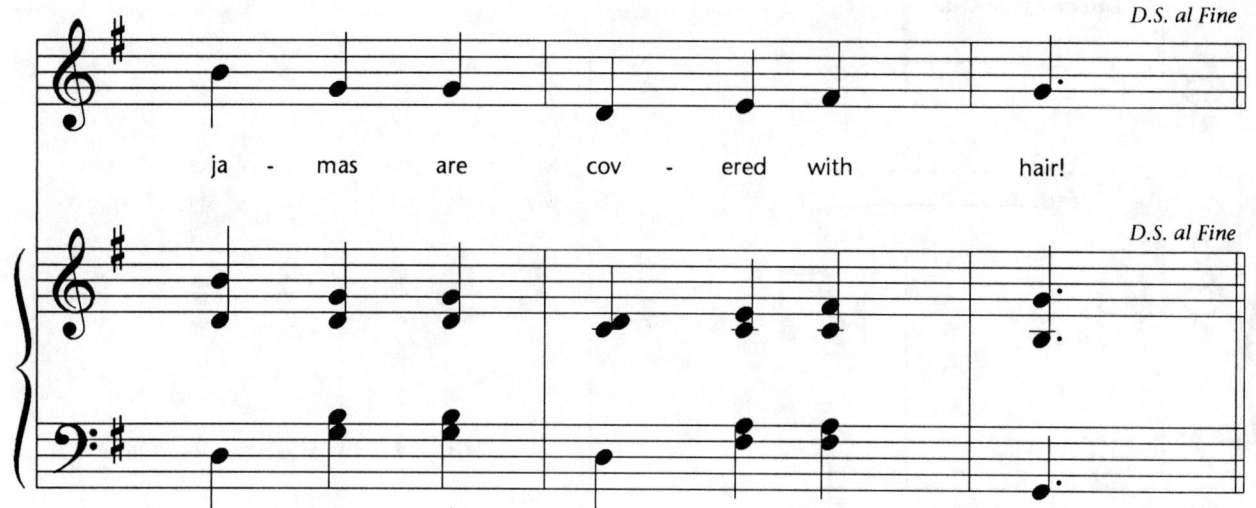

3. We told Uncle Walter that he should be good.
   And do all the things we say that he should,
   But I know he'd rather be off in the wood,
   We're afraid we will lose him, we'll lose him for good.
   Refrain

4. We said, "Uncle Walter, oh, please won't you stay,"
   And managed to keep him at home for a day,
   But the bears all barged in and they took him away,
   For the pandas demand at least one waltz a day!

   Refrain

5. Last night when the moon rose we crept down the stairs,
   He took me to dance where the bears have their lairs,
   We danced in a bear hug with nary a care, *(To Coda)*
   Refrain

Push the Business On

PUPIL'S PAGE 245

English Singing Game
Piano Accompaniment by Carol Jay

Comes Once In A Lifetime

PUPIL'S PAGE 252

Music by Jule Styne
Words by Betty Comden and Adolph Green
Piano Accompaniment by Carol Jay

146

I Can Be

PUPIL'S PAGE 254

Words and Music by Anthony Q. Richardson
Piano Accompaniment by Carol Jay

151

155

This Pretty Planet

PUPIL'S PAGE 257

Words and Music by John Forster and Tom Chapin

156

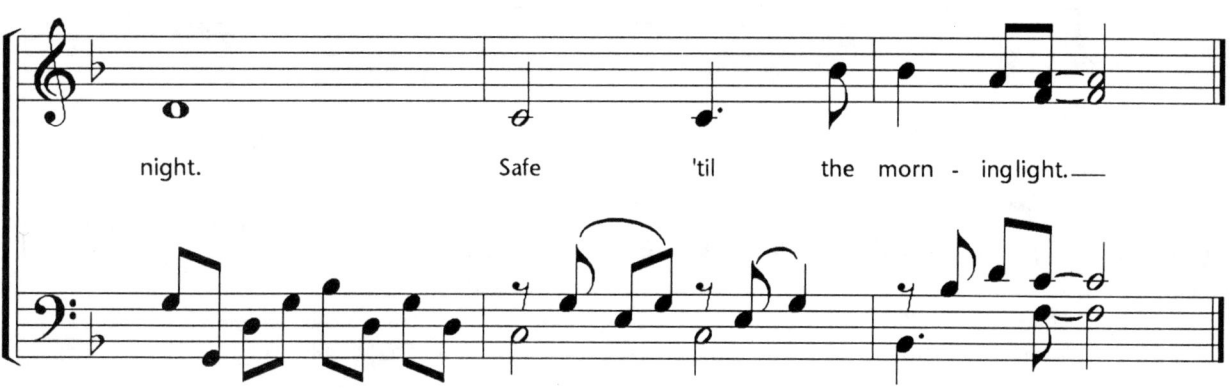

157

The Cat Came Back

PUPIL'S PAGE 258

American Folk Song
Arranged by Mary Goetze

3. He gave it to a man
   going up in a balloon.
   Told him to give it
   to the man up in the moon.
   The balloon came down
   about ninety miles away.
   What happened to the man?
   I really couldn't say.

   Refrain

4. A great tornado came
   just the other day.
   The wind began to blow,
   the trees began to sway.
   Thunder struck, lightning flashed,
   darkness took the day.
   The people were so frightened,
   they knelt right down to pray.

   Refrain

Old Joe Clark

PUPIL'S PAGE 260

American Folk Song
Piano Accompaniment by MMH

The Court of King Carraticus

PUPIL'S PAGE 263

American Nonsense Song
Piano Accompaniment by Carol Jay

verses accumulate

1. Oh, the court of King Car-ra-ti-cus is just pass-ing by; Oh, the
2. Oh, the pal-ace of the
   court of King Car-ra-ti-cus

court of King Car-ra-ti-cus is just pass-ing by; Oh, the
pal-ace of the
court of King Car-ra-ti-cus

From FIRESIDE BOOK OF FUN & GAME SONGS by Marie Winn and Alan Miller.
© 1974. Reprinted by permission of the publisher, Simon & Schuster, Inc., New York.

Add one phrase on each repetition of the song.
3. ladies of the palace of the court of King Carraticus are just passing by.
4. faces of the...
5. noses of the...
6. powder on the...
7. If you want to take a photo of the...
   (spoken at end) It's too late! They just passed by!

Michie Banjo

PUPIL'S PAGE 264

Creole Bamboula
English Words by Margaret Marks
Piano Accompaniment by Carol Jay

166

Simple Gifts

PUPIL'S PAGE 269

Shaker Song
Piano Accompaniment by MMH

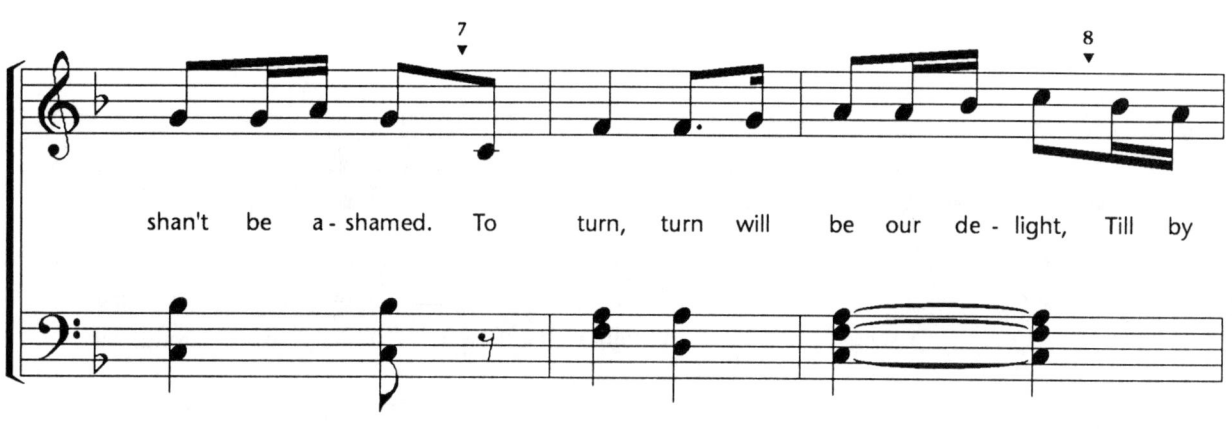

Garden Song

PUPIL'S PAGE 290

Words and Music by David Mallett
Piano Accompaniment by Kryste Andrews

170

Donna, Donna

PUPIL'S PAGE 291

Music by Sholom Secunda
Words by Aaron Zeitlen
Piano Accompaniment by Carol Jay

The Star-Spangled Banner

PUPIL'S PAGE 298

Music Attributed to J. S. Smith
Words by Francis Scott Key
Piano Accompaniment by MMH

America, the Beautiful

PUPIL'S PAGE 300

Music by Samuel Ward
Words by Katharine Lee Bates
Piano Accompaniment by MMH

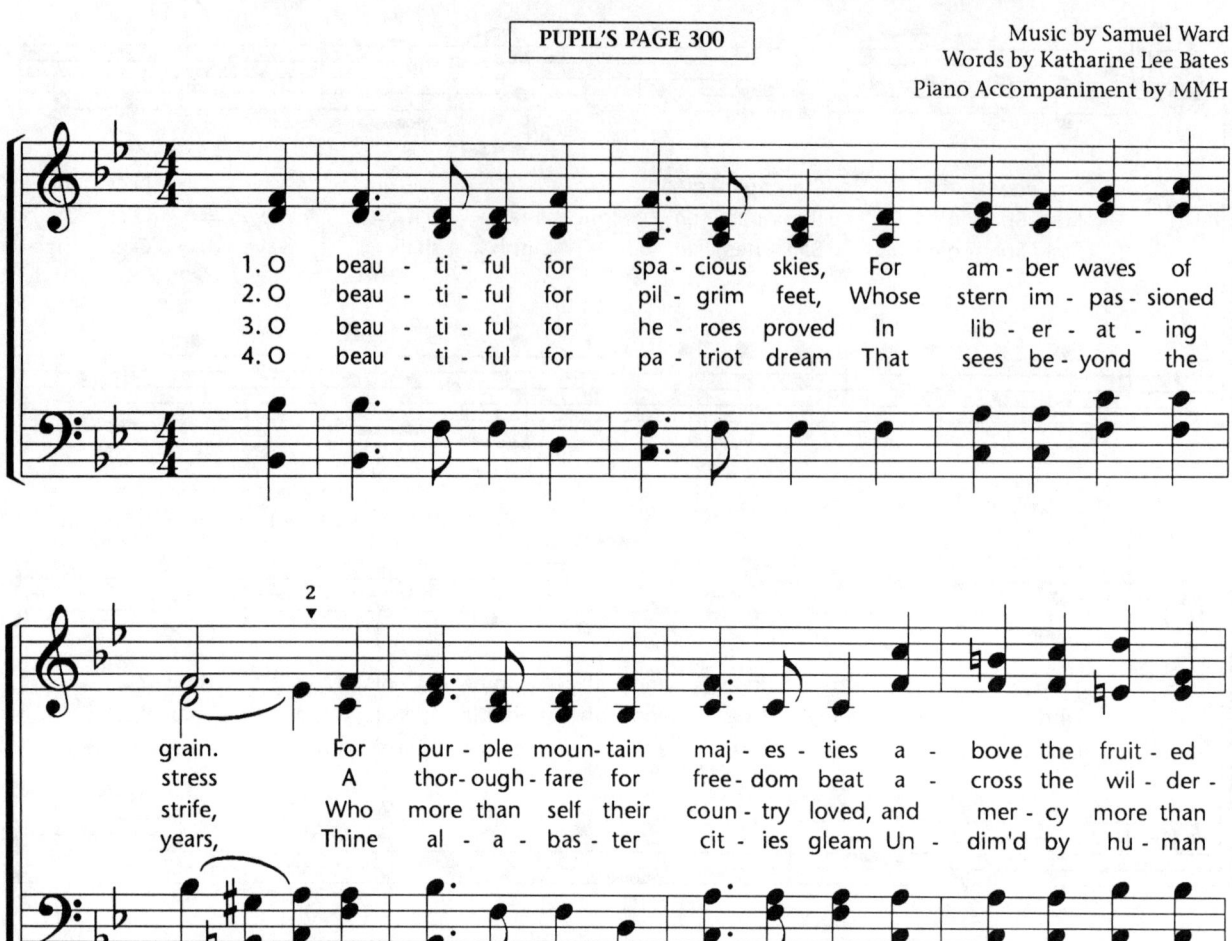

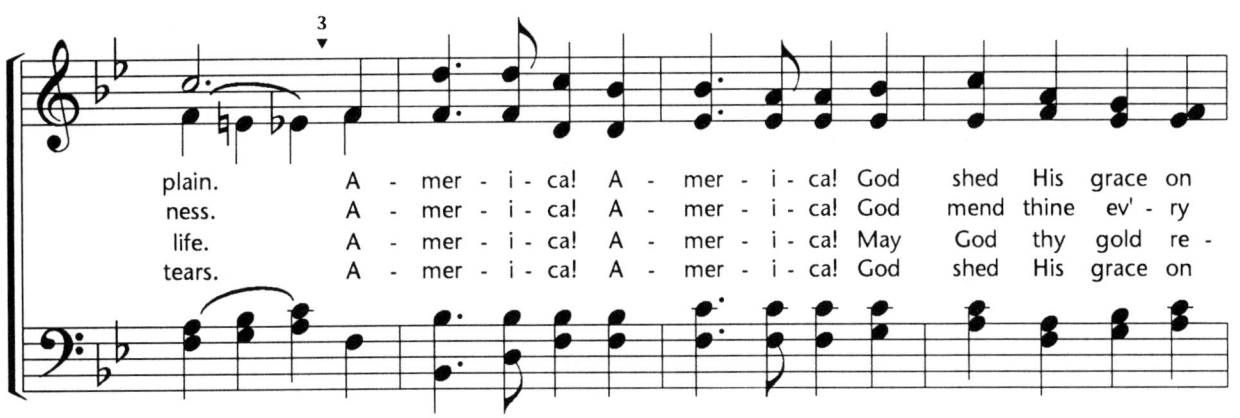
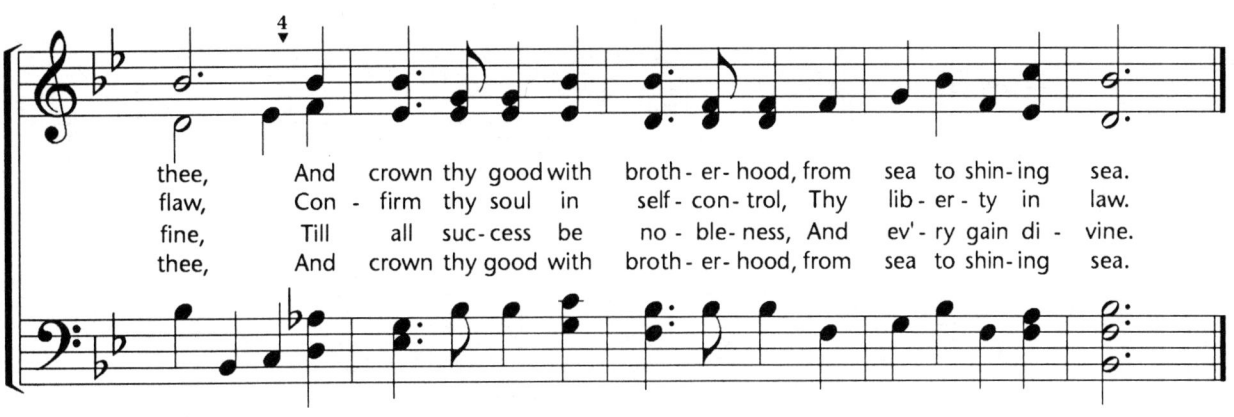

Sing a Song of Peace

PUPIL'S PAGE 301

Words and Music by Jill Gallina
Piano Accompaniment by Linda Worsley

America

PUPIL'S PAGE 302

Music by Henry Carey
Words by Samuel F. Smith
Piano Accompaniment by MMH

1. My country, 'tis of thee, Sweet land of liberty, Of thee I sing. Land where my fathers died, Land of the Pilgrim's pride, From ev'ry mountainside Let freedom ring.
2. My native country thee, Land of the noble free, Thy name I love. I love thy rocks and rills, Thy woods and templed hills; My heart with rapture thrills Like that above.
3. Let music swell the breeze, And ring from all the trees Sweet Freedom's song; Let mortal tongues awake, Let all that breathe partake, Let rocks their silence break, The sound prolong.
4. Our fathers' God, to Thee, Author of liberty, To Thee we sing. Long may our land be bright With Freedom's holy light; Protect us by Thy might, Great God, our King!

The Boogie Woogie Ghost

PUPIL'S PAGE 304

Words and Music by Nadine M. Peglar
Piano Accompaniment by Kryste Andrews

1. There was a ghost on Hal-low-een, He real-ly made the ghost-ie scene, He was the Boo-gie-Woo-gie Ghost, He was the ghost-ie with the most, And when the kid-dies came a-round, He'd give out
2. He'd go out spook-ing late at night, And giving ev'-ry-one a fright, He knew some wit-ches, two or three, And they would all go on a spree, And when the morn-ing came a-round, He'd give one

184

186

The Ghost Of John

PUPIL'S PAGE 306

Words and Music by Martha Grubb
Piano Accompaniment by Carol Jay

Dry Bones

PUPIL'S PAGE 308

African American Spiritual
Piano Accompaniment by Kryste Andrews

For Health and Strength

PUPIL'S PAGE 310

Old English Round
Piano Accompaniment by MMH

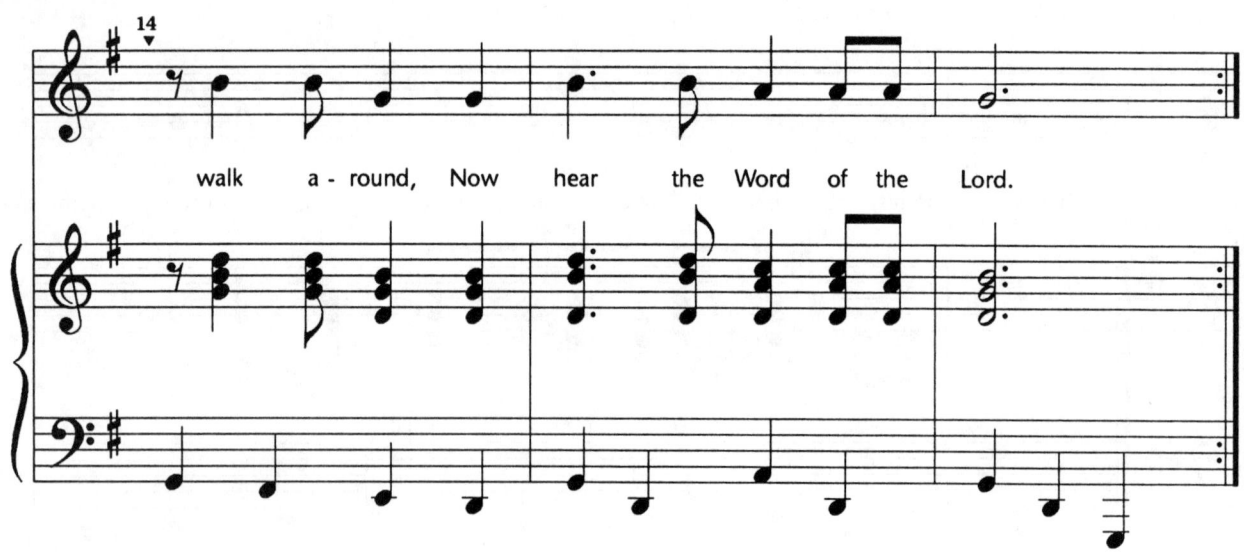

A Mince Pie or Pudding

PUPIL'S PAGE 311

Shaker Song
Piano Accompaniment by Ian Williams

Bonhomme! Bonhomme!

4. Can you play this on the great big horn?
   Ta-ta-ra on the great big horn, . . .

Winter Fantasy

PUPIL'S PAGE 314

Words and Music by Jill Gallina

197

198

201

In the Window

PUPIL'S PAGE 316

Hebrew Folk Song
Arranged by Mary Goetze
Piano Accompaniment by Bill and Pat Medley

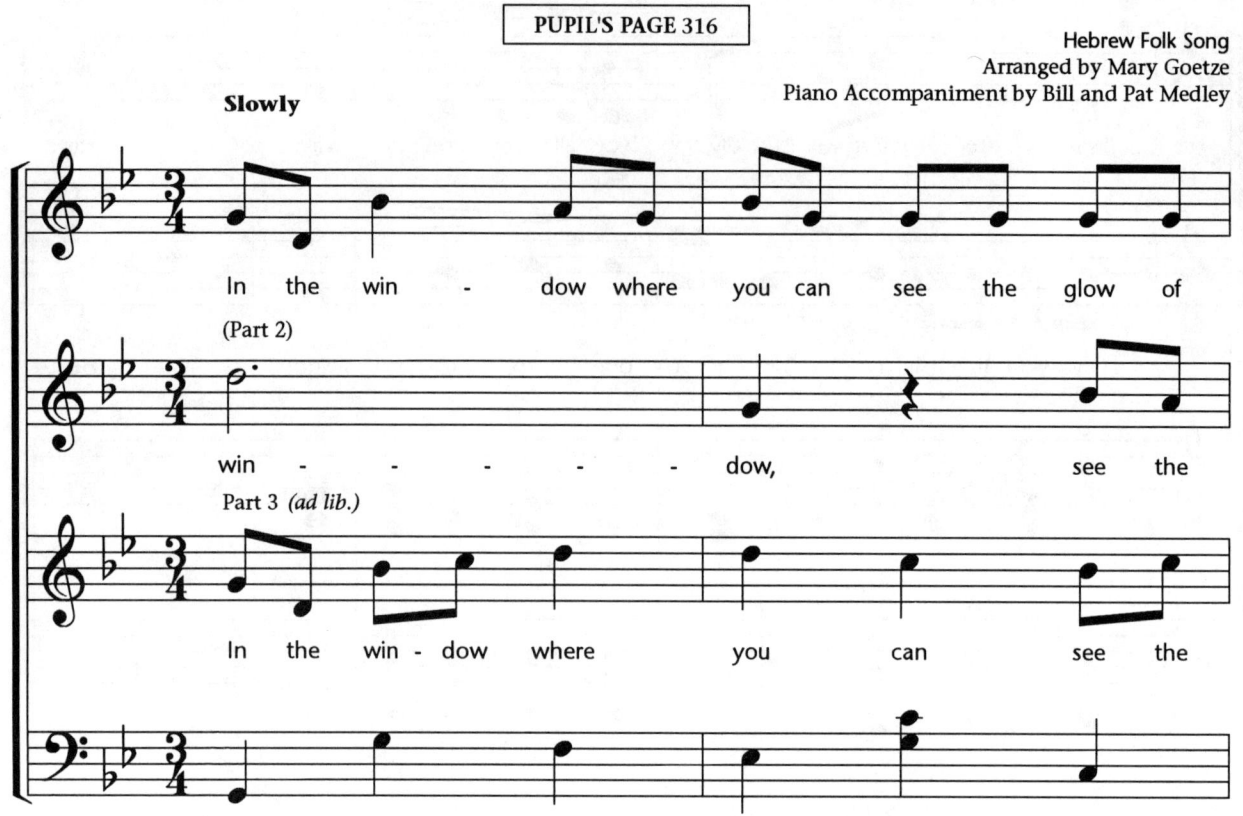

*On each of the nights of Hanukkah, sing the correct number.
On the eighth verse, sing the word "last."

Para pedir posada

PUPIL'S PAGE 318

Mexican Folk Song
English Version by MMH
Piano Accompaniment by Carol Jay

Entren santos peregrinos
Enter, Holy Pilgrims

PUPIL'S PAGE 321

Mexican Folk Song
English Version by MMH
Piano Accompaniment by Carol Jay

Dale, dale, dale!

PUPIL'S PAGE 322

Mexican Folk Song
Piano Accompaniment by Barbara Gastaldo

209

A Holly Jolly Christmas

PUPIL'S PAGE 324

Introduction not in Pupil's Edition Words and Music by Johnny Marks

213

O Tannenbaum!
O Christmas Tree!

PUPIL'S PAGE 326

German Carol
English Version by MMH
Piano Accompaniment by Bill and Pat Medley

German: O Tannenbaum, O Tannenbaum, wie treu sind deine Blätter! Du grünst nicht nur zur Sommerszeit, Nein, auch im Winter, wenn es schneit. O Tannenbaum, O Tannenbaum, wie treu sind deine Blätter!

English: O Tannenbaum, O Tannenbaum, your leaves are ever faithful! Not only green when summer glows, But in the winter when it snows. O Tannenbaum, O Tannenbaum, your leaves are ever faithful!

Somewhere In My Memory

PUPIL'S PAGE 327

Words by Leslie Bricusse
Music by John Williams
Piano Accompaniment by Steve Hoover

Can-dles in the win-dow, sha-dows paint-ing the ceil-ing,
gaz-ing at the fire glow, feel-ing that "gin-ger-bread" feel-ing.
Pre-cious mo-ments, spe-cial peo-ple, hap-py fac-es I can see.

pedal freely

215

Dormi, dormi
Sleep, Sleep

PUPIL'S PAGE 328

Italian Carol
English Text by George K. Evans
Piano Accompaniment by Mary Goetze

Italian: Dor - mi, dor - mi, bel bam - bin. Re di - vin,
English: Sleep, O sleep, my love - ly child. King di - vine,

We Three Kings

PUPIL'S PAGE 329

Words and Music by John Henry Hopkins
Piano Accompaniment by Bill and Pat Medley

The Twelve Days of Christmas

PUPIL'S PAGE 330

English Carol
Piano Accompaniment by Bill and Pat Medley

7. ...Seven swans a-swimming,...
8. ...Eight maids a-milking,...
9. ...Nine drummers drumming,...
10. ...Ten pipers piping,...
11. ...Eleven ladies dancing,...
12. ...Twelve lords a-leaping,...

Suk san wan pi mai
New Year's Song

PUPIL'S PAGE 333

Laotian Song
Collected and Transcribed by Kathy B. Sorensen
English Version by MMH
Piano Accompaniment by Carol Jay

Martin's Cry

PUPIL'S PAGE 336

Words and Music by Vernon Clark

Down By The Riverside

PUPIL'S PAGE 338

African American Spiritual
Piano Accompaniment by Bill and Pat Medley

234

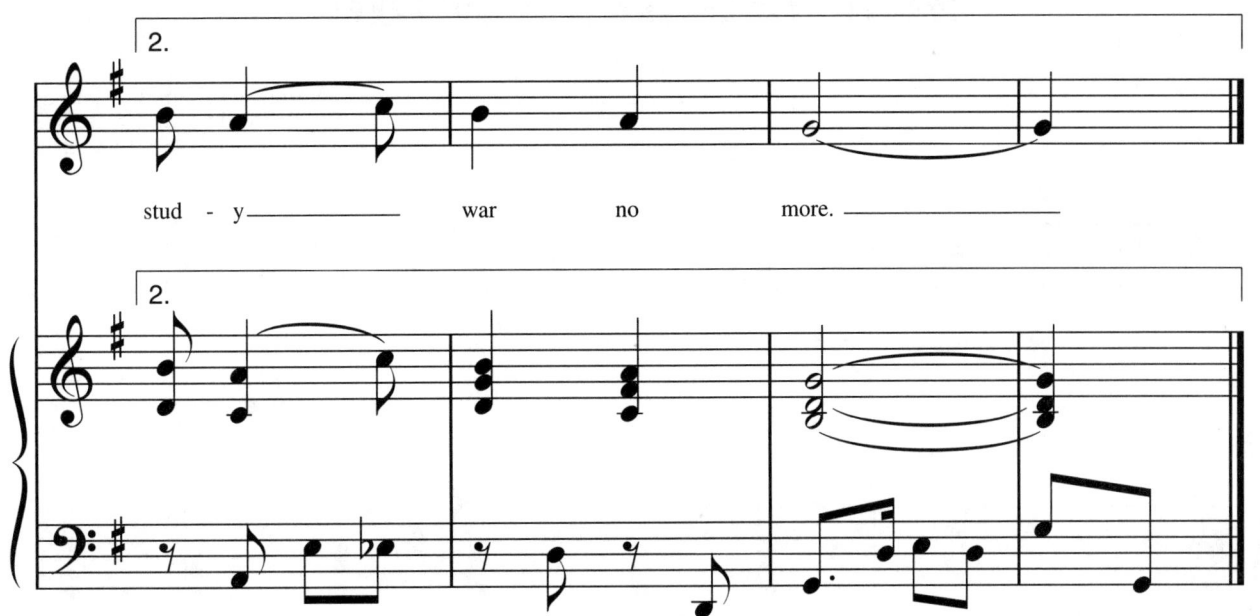

Macnamara's Band

PUPIL'S PAGE 342

Music by Shamus O'Connor
Words by John J. Stamford
Piano Accompaniment by Bill and Pat Medley

1. Oh! me name is Mac-na-mar-a, I'm the lead-er of the band, Al-though we're few in num-bers we're the fin-est in the
2. Right now we are re-hears-in', for a ver-y swell af-fair, The an-nual cel-e-bra-tion, all the gen-try will be
3. Oh! my name is Un-cle Yul-ius and from Swe-den I have come, To play with Mac-na-mar-a's band and beat the big bass
4. Oh! I wear a bunch of sham-rocks and a un-i-form of green, And I'm the fun-niest look-ing Swede that you have ev-er

Tree Song

PUPIL'S PAGE 344

Words and Music by Ken Medema
Piano Accompaniment by Linda Worsley

1. I saw a tree by the river-side one day as I walked a-long.
2. I saw a tree in the winter time when snow lay on the ground.
3. I saw a tree in the city streets where buildings blocked the sun.

Straight as an arrow and pointing to the sky,
Straight as an arrow and pointing to the sky, and
Green and lovely I could see it gave

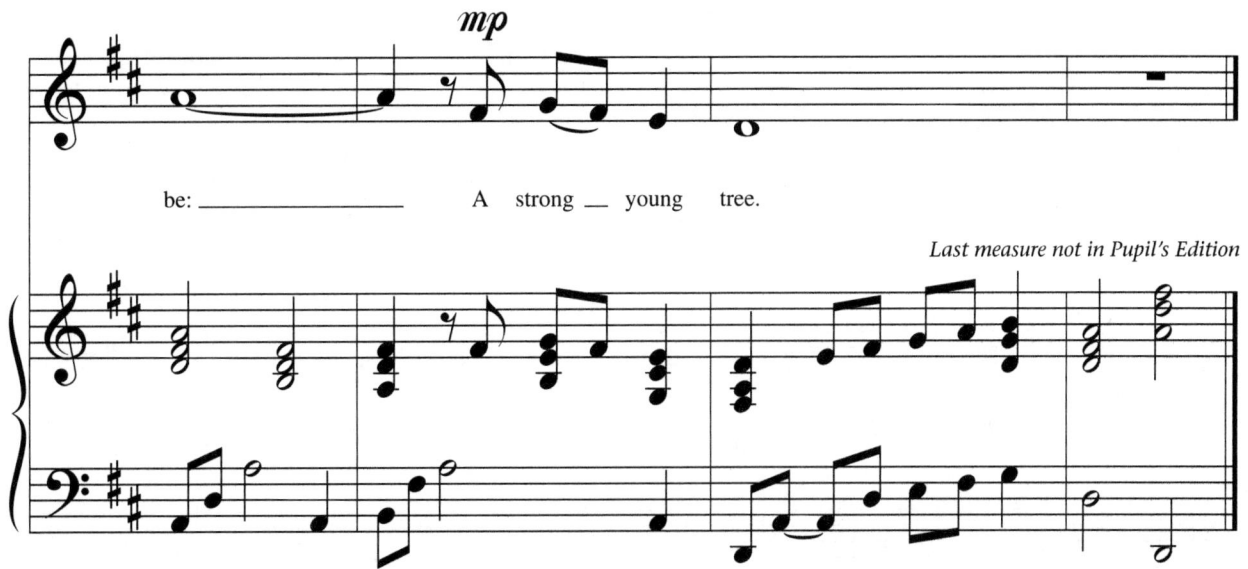

I Love the Mountains

PUPIL'S PAGE 346

Traditional Round
Piano Accompaniment by Ian Williams

I love the moun - tains, I love the roll - ing hills,

I love the flow - ers, I love the daf - fo - dils;

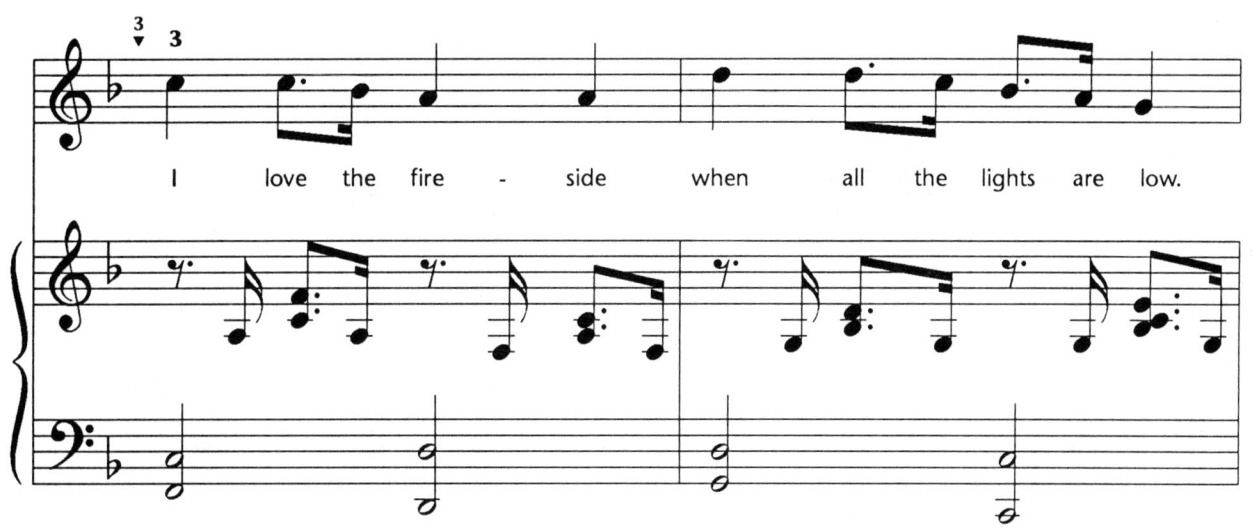

Night Song

PUPIL'S PAGE 347

German Folk Song
Piano Accompaniment by Carol Jay

Go 'Round the Mountain

PUPIL'S PAGE 347

Illinois Play Party Song
Piano Accompaniment by Marilyn Christensen

4. Girls through the window; . . .

5. Boys through the window; . . .

6. Find you a new love; . . .

Babylon's Fallin'

PUPIL'S PAGE 348

Virginia Folk Song
Piano Accompaniment by Carol Jay

Page's Train

PUPIL'S PAGE 349

North Carolina Folk Song
Piano Accompaniment by Carol Jay

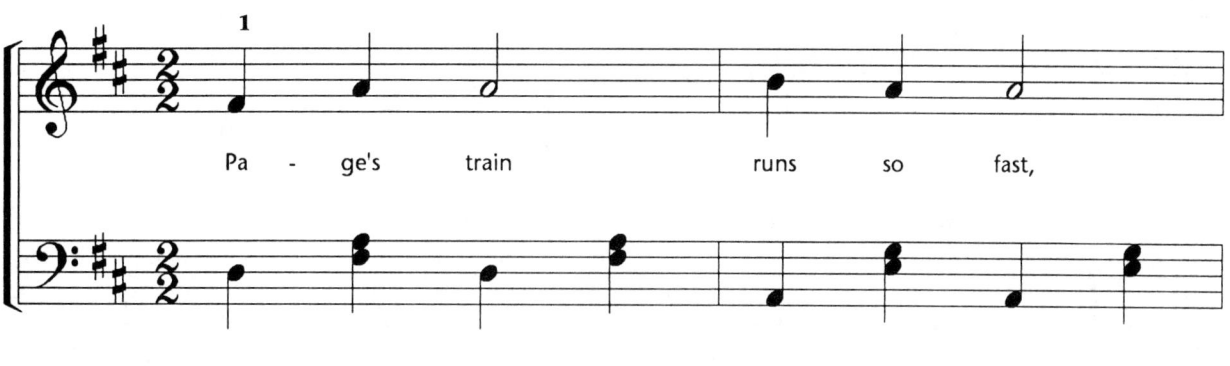

I Am a Cat

PUPIL'S PAGE 349

Music by Marilyn Copeland Davidson
Anonymous Poem
Piano Accompaniment by Steve Hoover

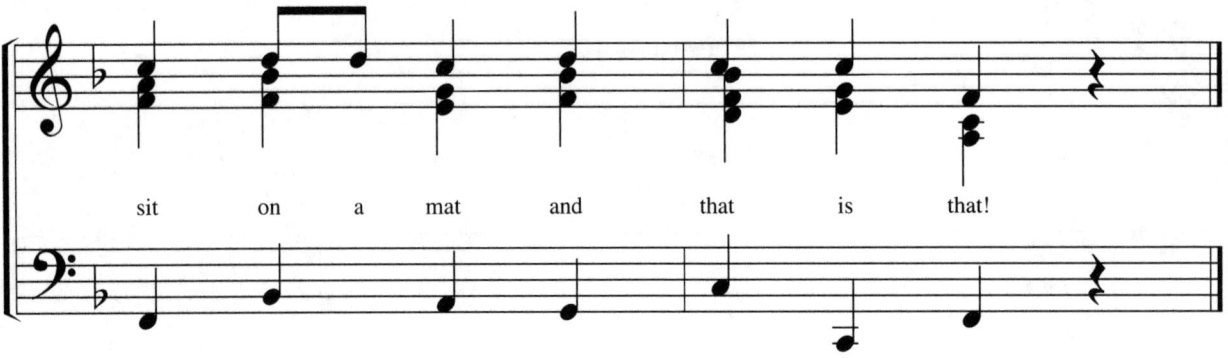

Lady, Come Down and See

PUPIL'S PAGE 350

Traditional Round
Piano Accompaniment by Carol Jay

La - dy, come down and see, the cat sits in the plum tree.

Dinah

PUPIL'S PAGE 351

American Minstrel Song
Piano Accompaniment by Linda Worsley

Ida Red

PUPIL'S PAGE 352

Kentucky Folk Song
Piano Accompaniment by Carol Jay

Refrain

Down the road and a-cross the creek,

Can't get a let-ter but once a week.

255

The Old Chisholm Trail

PUPIL'S PAGE 354

Cowboy Song
Piano Accompaniment by Carol Jay

2. I woke one mornin' on the old Chisholm trail,
   A rope in my hand and cow by the tail. *Refrain*

3. I started up the trail on October twenty-third,
   Started up the trail with the old cow herd. *Refrain*

4. On a ten dollar horse and a forty dollar saddle,
   I'm gonna puch those Texas cattle. *Refrain*

5. It's bacon and beans 'most ev'ry day,
   I'd as soon be a-eatin' prairie hay. *Refrain*

6. It's cloudy in the west and it looks like rain,
   And I left my old slicker in the wagon again. *Refrain*

7. I'm gonna see the boss, gonna get my money,
   Goin' back home to see my honey. *Refrain*

Old Tar River

PUPIL'S PAGE 355

American Folk Song
Piano Accompaniment by William N. Simon

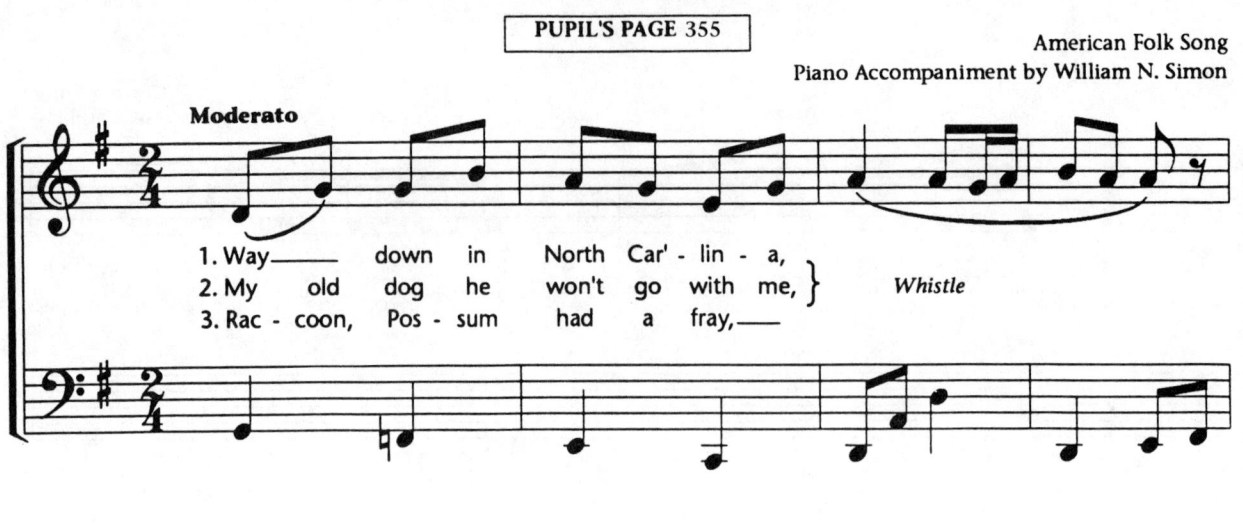

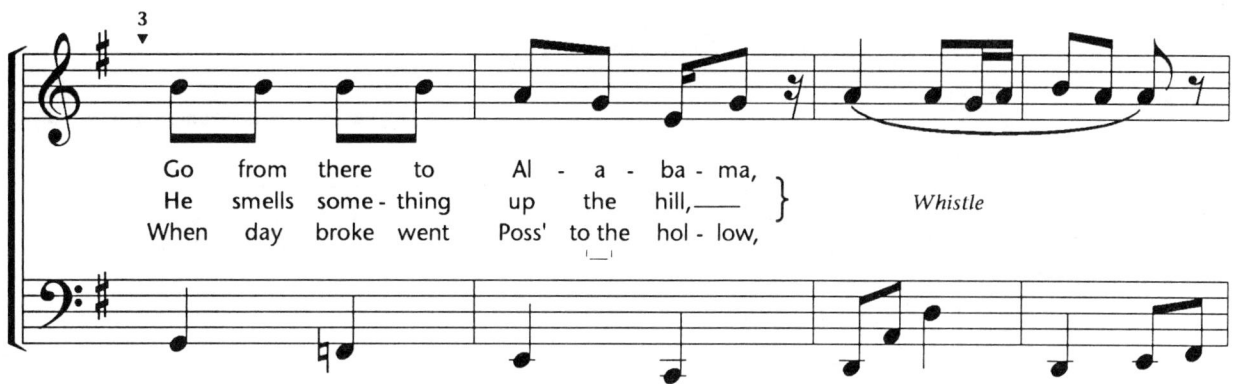

4. Old dog watch, smelled all around,
   Found Raccoon just left the ground,
   Then he bark right up the tree,
   Raccoon says, "You can't catch me."

5. Dinah, I am going to leave you;
   When I'm gone don't let it grieve you,
   First to the window, then to the door,
   Looking for to see my banjo.

Heave-Ho Me Laddies

PUPIL'S PAGE 356

Sea Chantey
Piano Accompaniment by Carol Jay

Oh if I were a sail-or out a sail-ing on the sea,_____ I real-ly am quite cer-tain_____ a cap-tain I would be. Heave - ho me

My Horses Ain't Hungry

PUPIL'S PAGE 357

Tennessee Folk Song
Piano Accompaniment by Bill and Pat Medley

Introduction not in Pupil's Edition

1. My horses ain't hungry, They won't eat your hay, So I'll get on my pony, I'm going away.
2. I know you're my Polly, I'm not going to stay, So come with me darling, We'll feed on our way.
3. With all our belongings, We'll ride till we come To a lonely cabin, We'll call it our home.

The Derby Ram

PUPIL'S PAGE 358

English Folk Song
Ozark Version
Piano Accompaniment by Carol Jay

4. The ears upon this ram's head
   They reached to the sky,
   the eagle built his nest there,
   For I heard the young ones cry.

   Refrain

5. Oh ev'ry tooth this ram had
   would hold a bushel of corn,
   And ev'ry foot he stood on,
   Would cover an acre of ground.

   Refrain

Lots o' Fish in Bonavist' Harbor

Newfoundland Folk Song
Piano Accompaniment by William S. Simon

Old Dan Tucker

PUPIL'S PAGE 360

American Folk Song
Folk version of Dan Emmett's minstrel song
Piano Accompaniment by William M. Simon

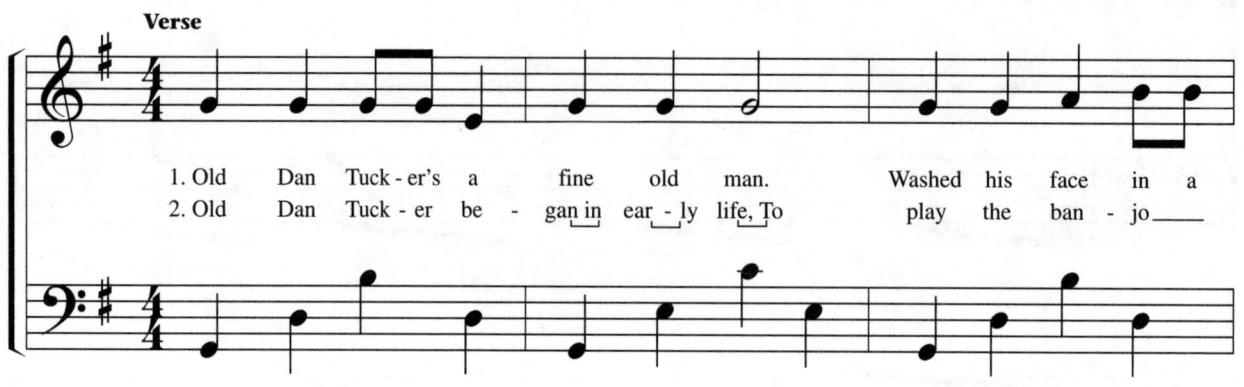

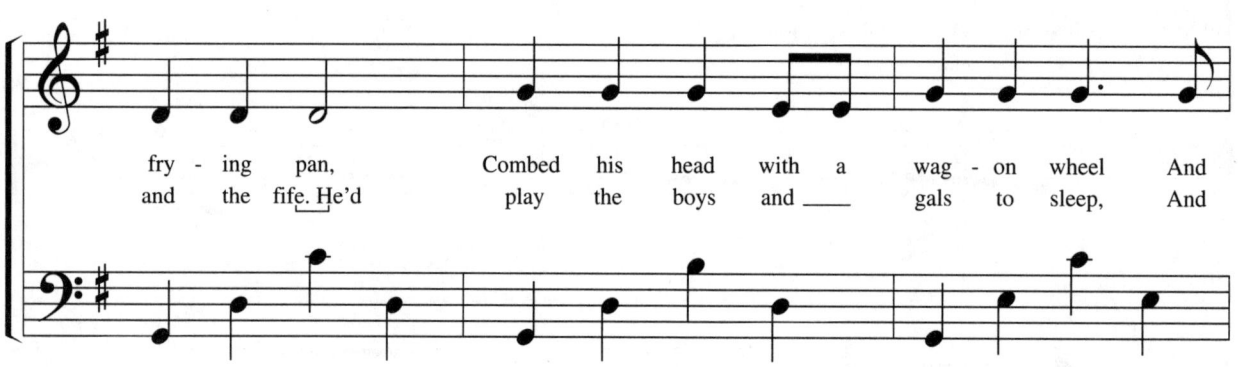

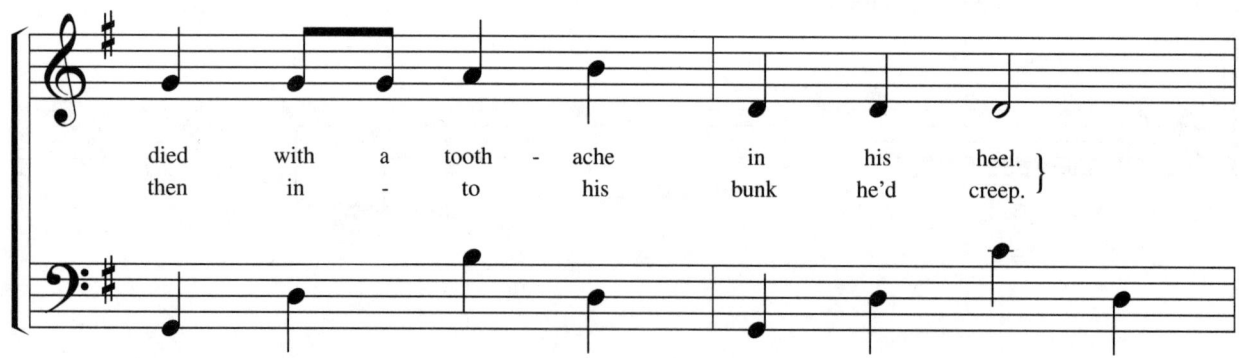

My Dame Hath a Lame, Tame Crane

PUPIL'S PAGE 361

Traditional English Round
Piano Accompaniment by MMH

To Stop the Train

PUPIL'S PAGE 361

English Round
Piano Accompaniment by Carol Jay

Before Dinner

PUPIL'S PAGE 362

Zairian Folk Song
Piano Accompaniment by Carol Jay

First we go to hoe our gar-den, } Ya, ya, ya, ya.
Next we car-ry jugs of wa-ter,

Then we pound the yel-low corn, } Ya, ya, ya, ya.
Then we stir our pots of mush,

Now we eat, come gath-er 'round the camp-fire, Ya, ya, ya, ya.

Hop Up and Jump Up

PUPIL'S PAGE 363

Shaker Song
Piano Accompaniment by Carol Jay

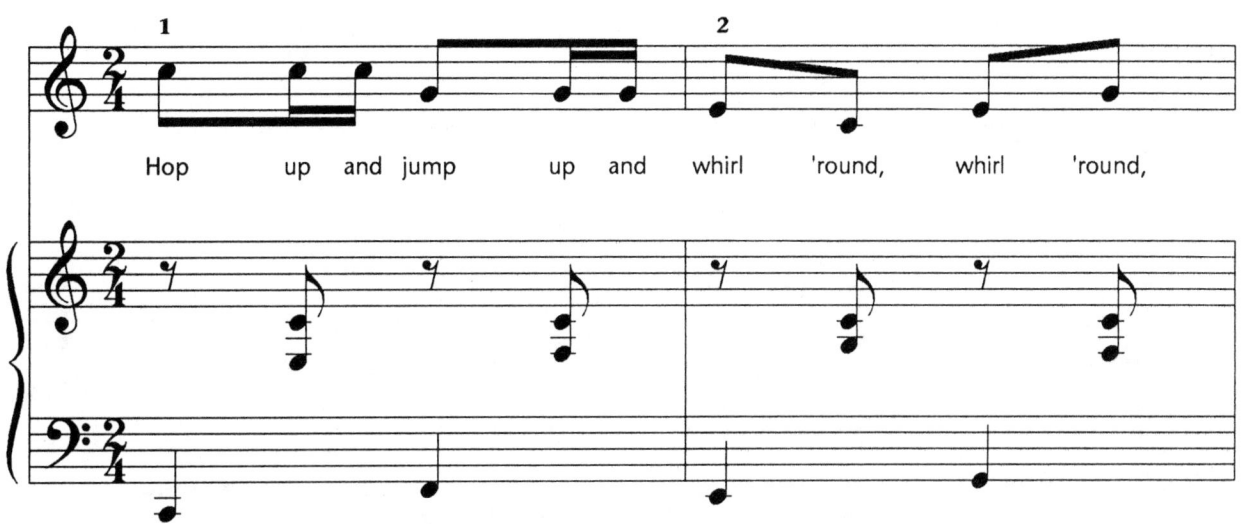

Oliver Cromwell

PUPIL'S PAGE 364

English Folk Song
Piano Accompaniment by Benjamin Britten

1. Oliver Cromwell lay buried and dead, Hee haw, buried and dead. There grew an old apple tree
(2.) apples were ripe and ready to fall, Hee haw, ready to fall. There came an old woman to
(3.) saddle and bridle, they lie on the shelf, Hee haw, lie on the shelf. If you want any more you can

Who's Got a Fishpole?

PUPIL'S PAGE 364

American Song
Piano Accompaniment by John Richards

277

280

Alleluia, Amen

PUPIL'S PAGE 366

Traditional Round
Piano Accompaniment by Linda Worsley

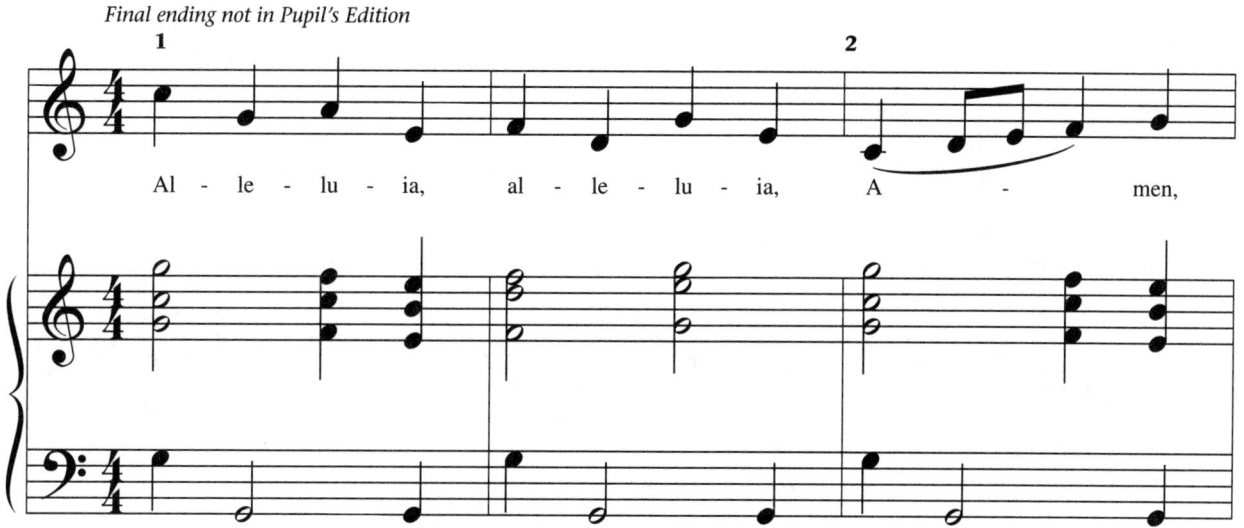

San lun tsa
Three-Wheeled Taxi

PUPIL'S PAGE 366

Taiwanese Folk Song
Collected and Transcribed by Kathy B. Sorensen
English Version by MMH
Piano Accompaniment by Carol Jay

John Kanaka

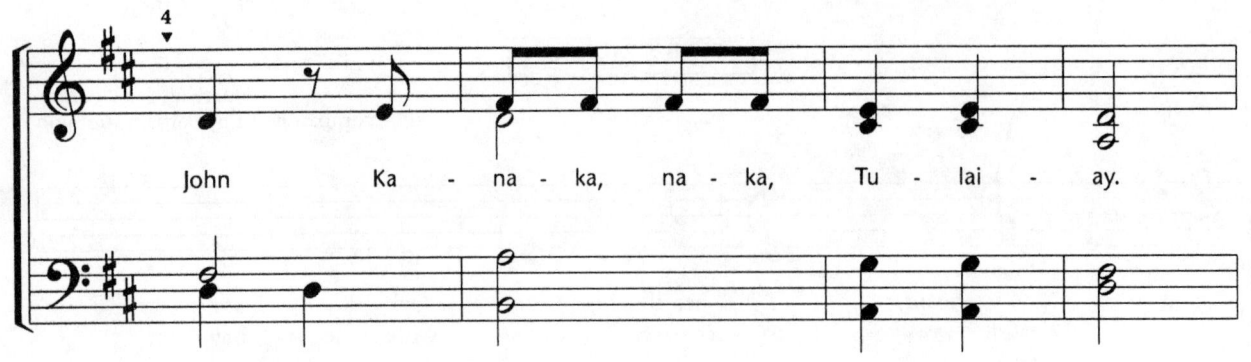

4. A Yankee ship wid a Yankee crew, . . .
    Oh, we're the buckos fer to push 'er through. . . .

5. Oh, haul away, oh, haul away! . . .
    Oh, haul away, an' make your pay. . . .

Ah, Poor Bird

PUPIL'S PAGE 368

Old English Melody
Piano Accompaniment by Carol Jay

1. Ah, poor bird, take your flight,
Far above the sorrows of this sad night.

2. Ah, poor bird, as you fly,
Can you see the dawn of tomorrow's sky?

From GROWING WITH MUSIC, Book 3 TE, by Wilson et al.
© 1970 Prentice-Hall, Inc., Englewood Cliffs, NJ. Arrangement adapted.

Chickalileeo

PUPIL'S PAGE 368

Southern Folk Song
Piano Accompaniment by Linda Worsley

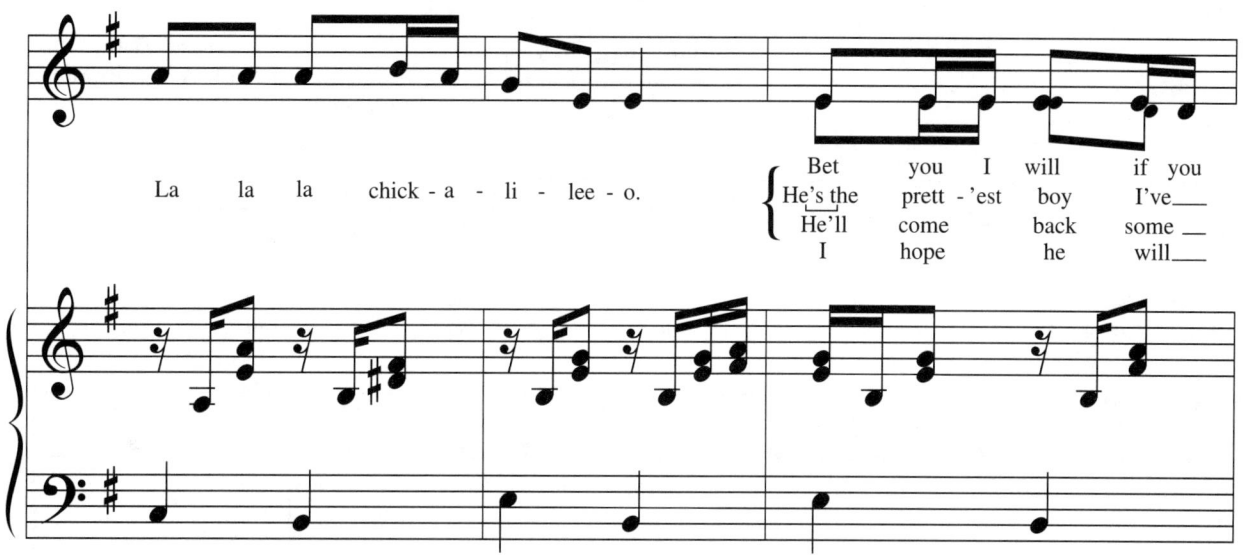

287

Artsa Alinu
Our Land

PUPIL'S PAGE 369

Israeli Dance Song
English Version by MMH
Piano Accompaniment by Anna Marie Spallina

Korobushka

PUPIL'S PAGE 370

Russian Folk Song
Russian Words by Nikolay Kekrasov
English Version by MMH
Piano Accompaniment by Carol Jay

289

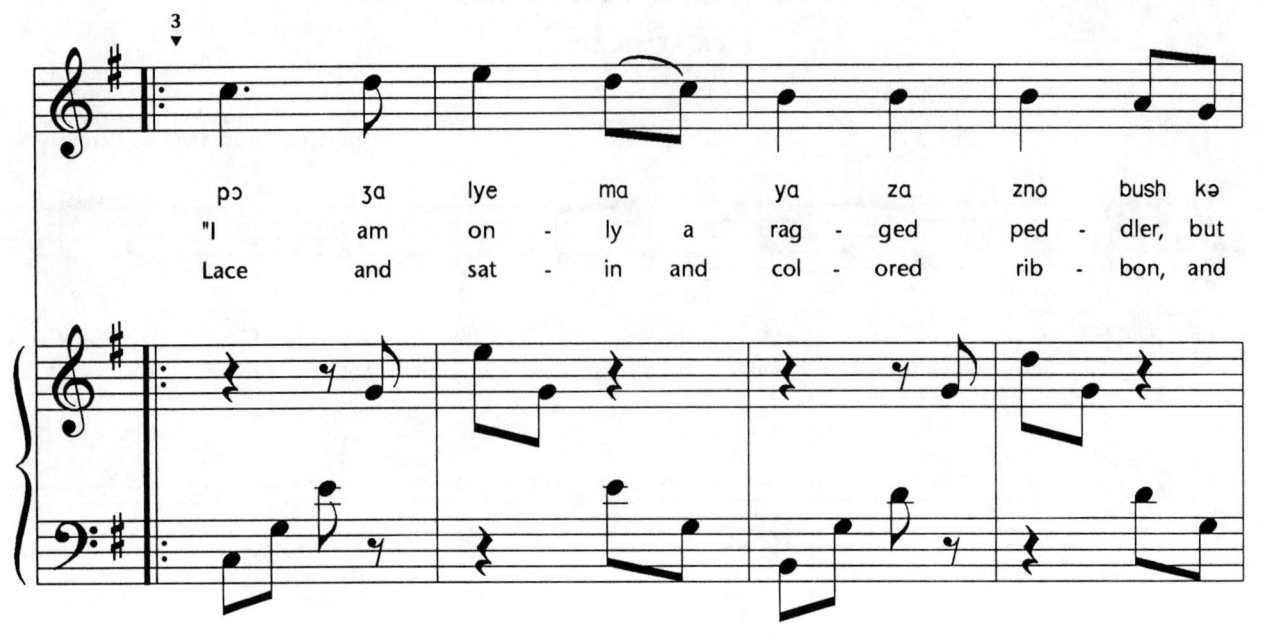
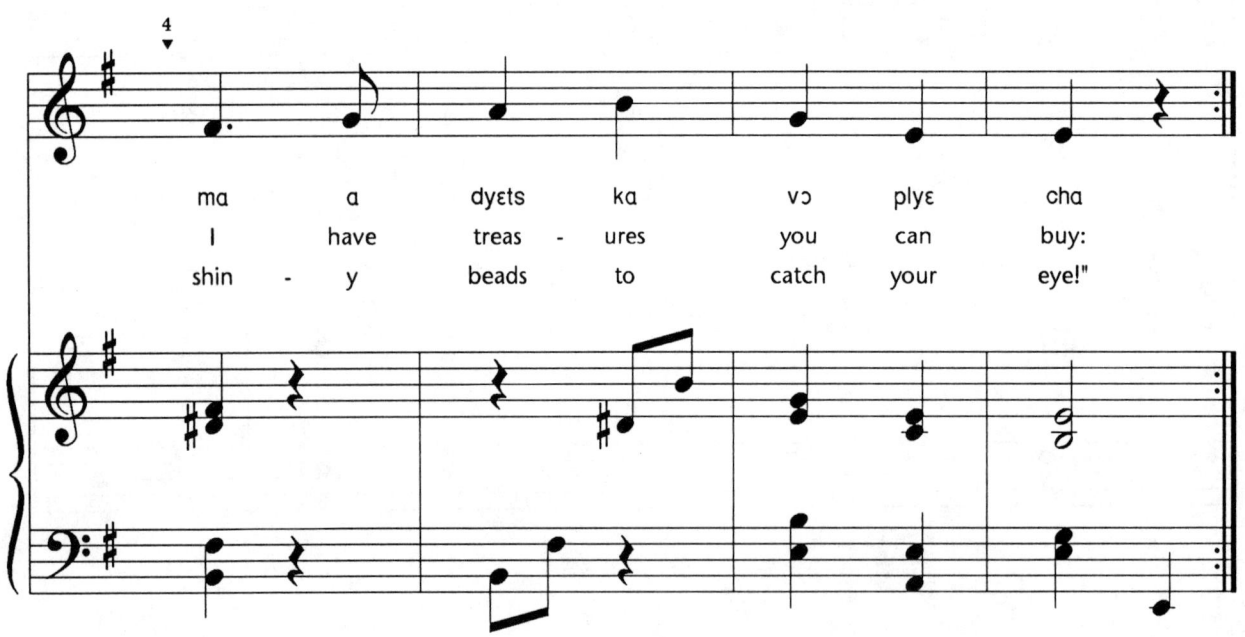

O musique

PUPIL'S PAGE 371

French Folk Song
English Version by MMH
Piano Accompaniment by Bill and Pat Medley

291

Alouette

PUPIL'S PAGE 371

French Canadian Folk Song
English Version by MMH
Piano Accompaniment by MMH

3. Le nez

4. Le dos

5. Les pattes

6. Le cou

The Path to the Moon

PUPIL'S PAGE 372

Music by Eric H. Thiman
Words by Madeline C. Thomas
Piano Accompaniment by Linda Worsley

293

car - ry me o - ver the sea.

295

Haida

PUPIL'S PAGE 375

Hassidic Round
Arranged by Henry Leck
Piano Accompaniment by Carol Jay

And Where Is Home?

PUPIL'S PAGE 378

Words and Music by Margaret Campbelle-Holman

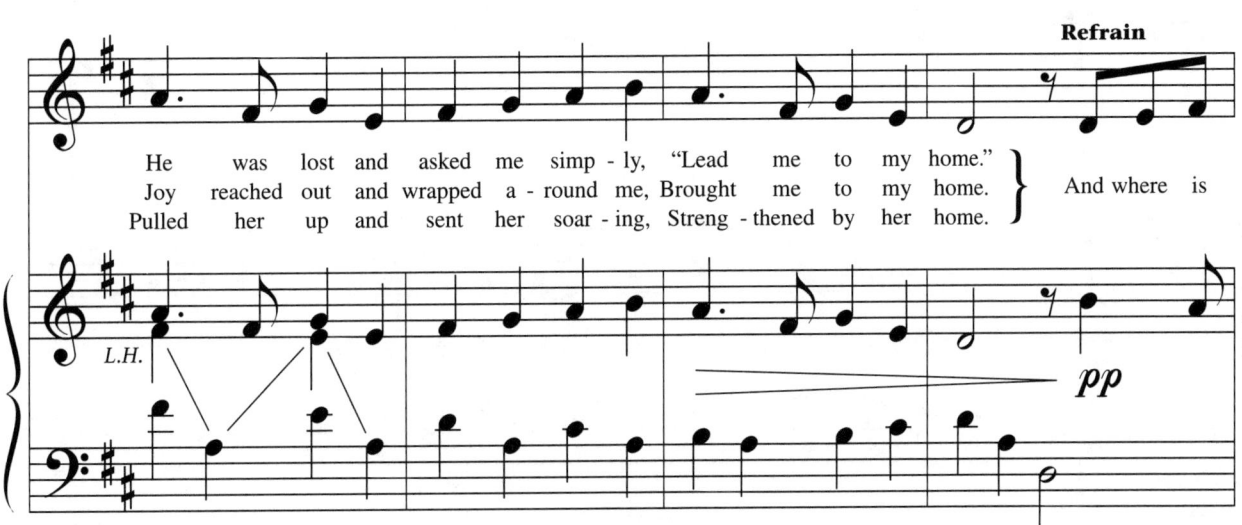

303

Don't Let the Music Stop II

PUPIL'S PAGE 380

Words and Music by Eugene Butler
Piano Accompaniment by Linda Worsley

Introduction not in Pupil's Edition

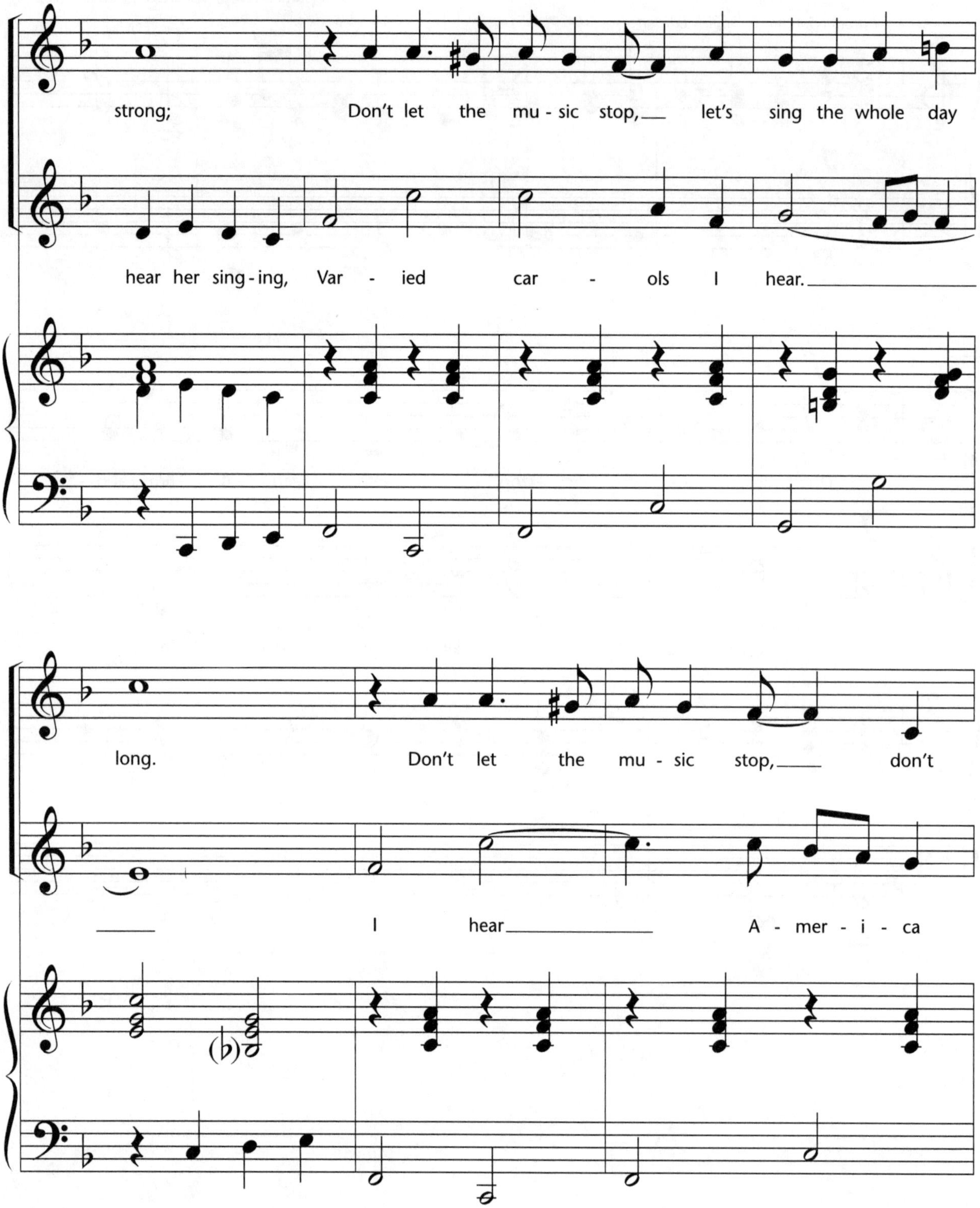
strong; Don't let the mu - sic stop,___ let's sing the whole day
hear her sing - ing, Var - ied car - ols I hear.___
long. Don't let the mu - sic stop,___ don't
___ I hear___ A - mer - i - ca

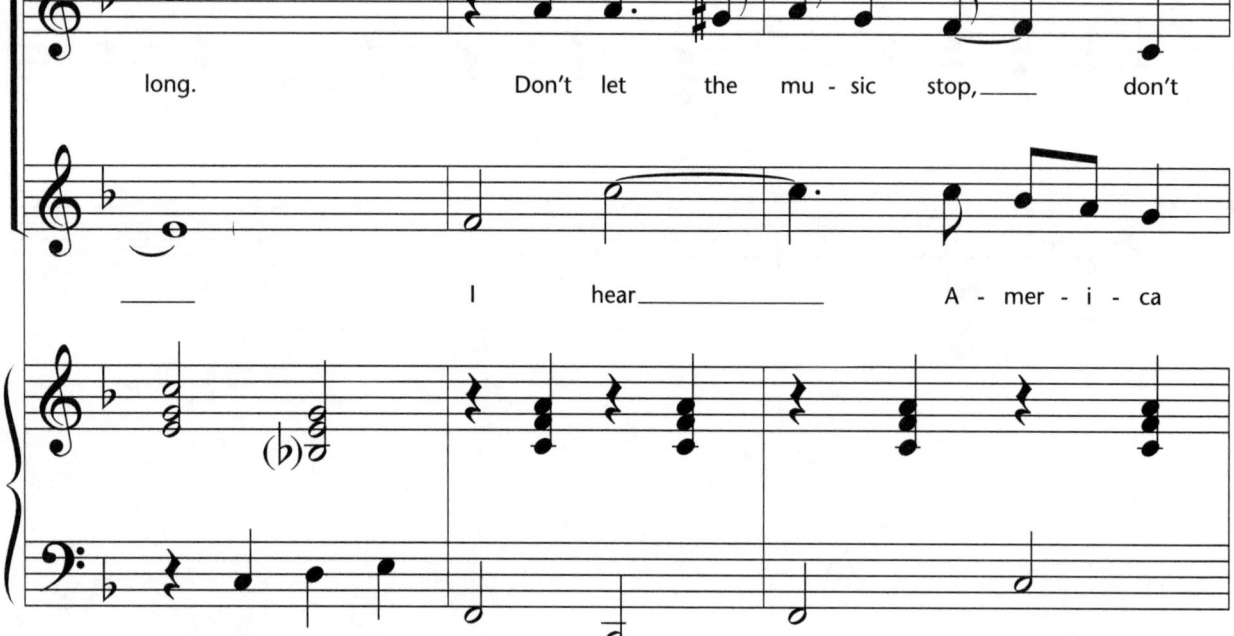

Happiness

PUPIL'S PAGE 386

Words and Music by Linda Worsley

Introduction not in Pupil's Edition

I *Chorus:* Hap - pi - ness, And ad - ven - ture, What a great sen - sa - tion!
II *Ned:* Hap - pi - ness, And ad - ven - ture, What a great sen - sa - tion!
III *Ned:* Hap - pi - ness, And con - tent - ment! What a fine sen - sa - tion!

311

No Matter What

PUPIL'S PAGE 388

*I: First time Traveler and Ned;
on repeat, Chorus, with Ned and
Traveler on echo phrases.*

Introduction not in Pupil's Edition

Words and Music by Linda Worsley

317

Things That Grow

PUPIL'S PAGE 390

*First time Farmer;
on repeat, Chorus, with
Farmer on echo phrases.
Introduction and Coda not in Pupil's Edition*

Words and Music by Linda Worsley

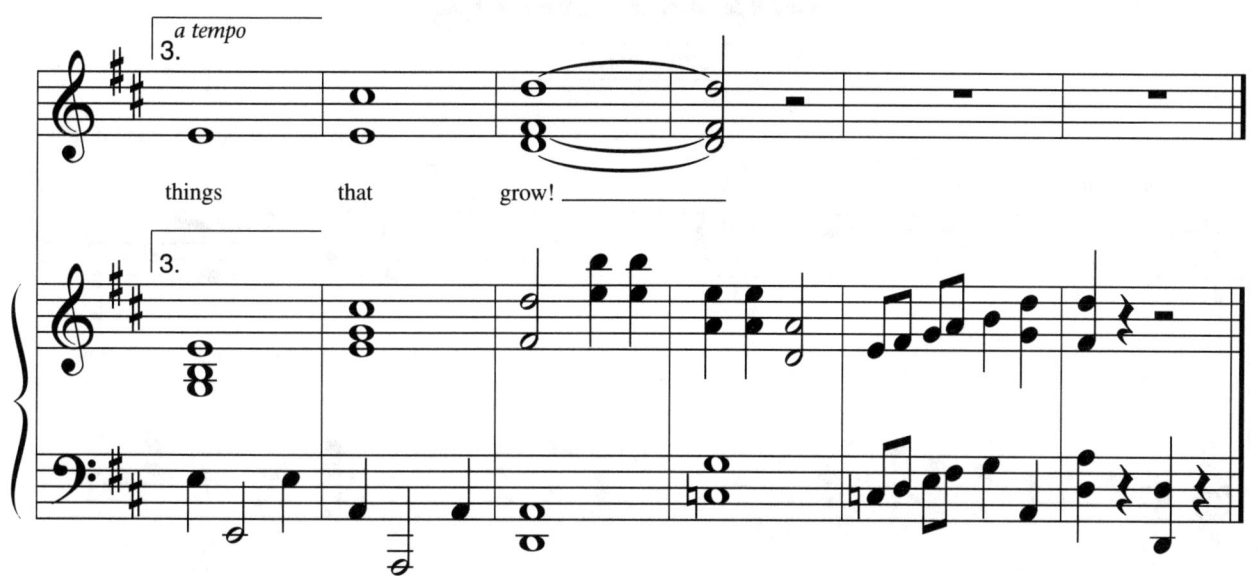

325

Barter Song

PUPIL'S PAGE 392

Words and Music by Linda Worsley

Bird in the Water

PUPIL'S PAGE 393

Words and Music by Linda Worsley

333

Stone Pounding

PUPIL'S PAGE 160

Jamaican Folk Song
Transcribed by Helen H. Roberts
Piano Accompaniment by Carol Jay

336

At the Hop

PUPIL'S PAGE HL2

Words and Music by Arthur Singer,
John Madara and David White
Piano Accompaniment by Mark Brymer

Divide the cast into four equal groups. In the first 8 bars of singing, there will be a peel-off move that each group does in succession starting with the group furthest stage L. Each "Ba" has a move by one of the groups.

Introduction not in Pupil's Edition

338

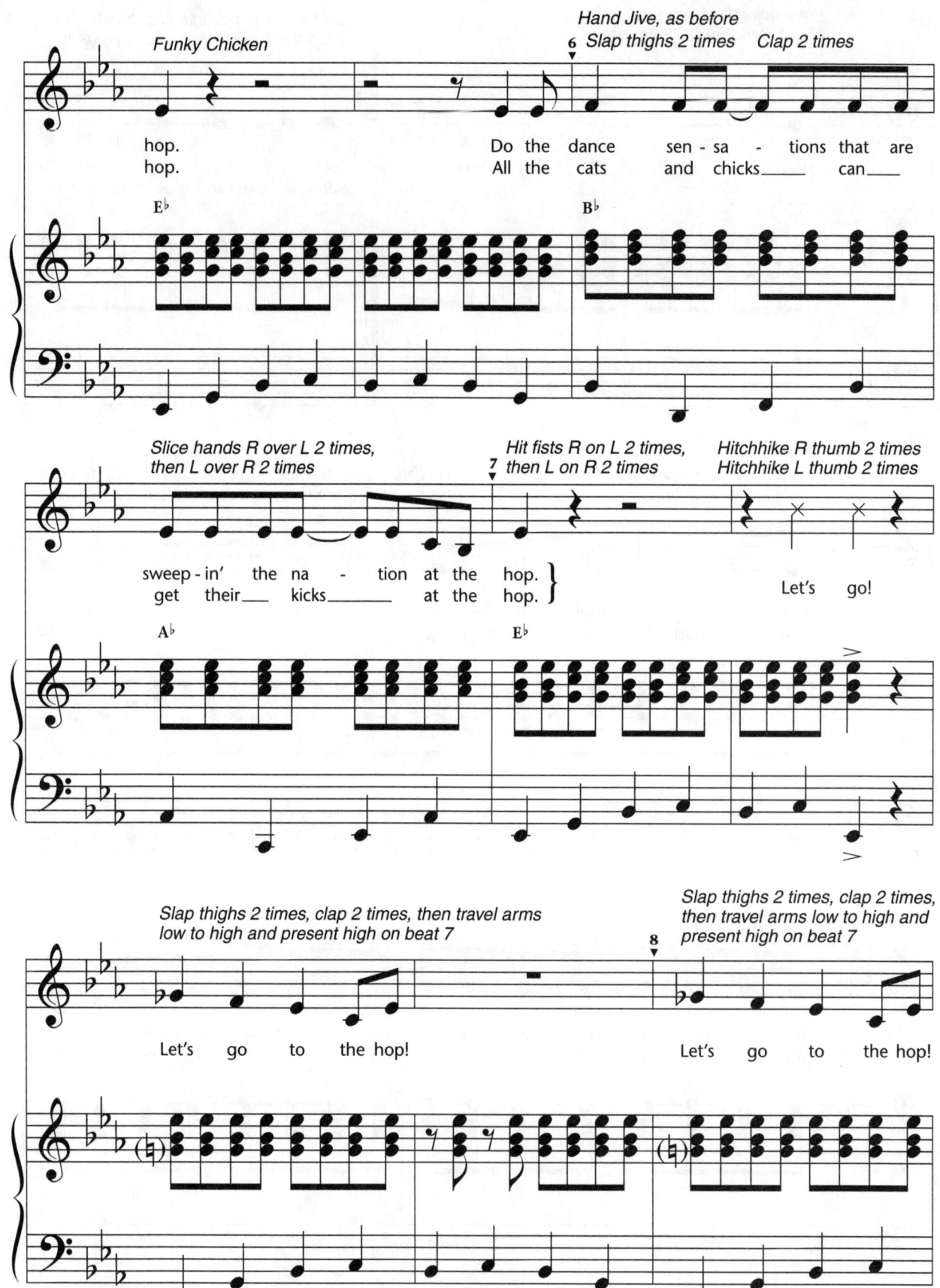

Dancing in the Street

PUPIL'S PAGE HL4

Words and Music by Arthur Singer,
John Madara and David White
Piano Accompaniment by Mark Brymer

We Got the Beat

PUPIL'S PAGE HL6

Words and Music by Charlotte Caffey
Piano Accompaniment by Mark Brymer

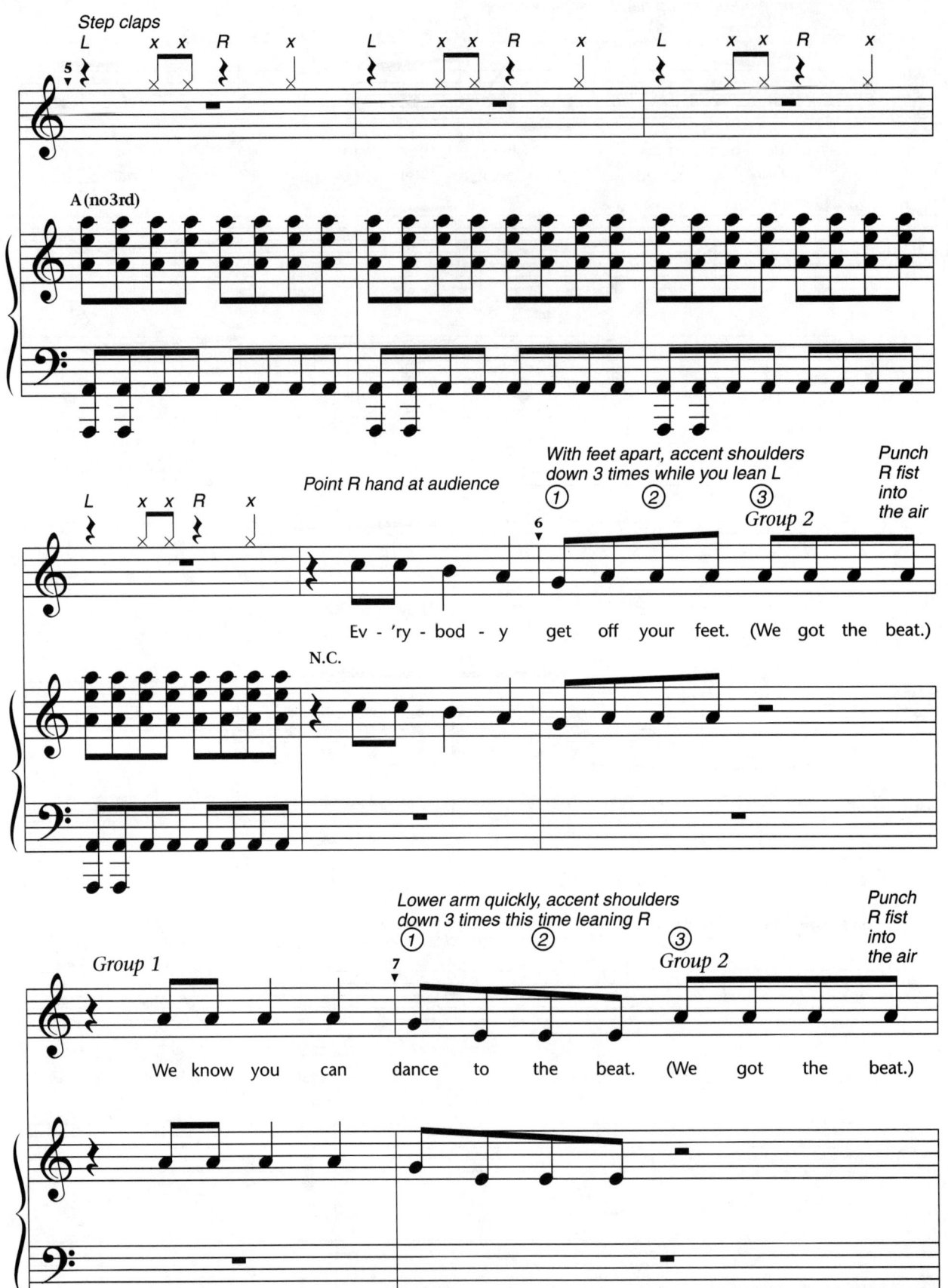

The Loco-Motion

PUPIL'S PAGE HL8

Words and Music by
Gerry Goffin and Carole King
Piano Accompaniment by Mark Brymer

Bristol Stomp

PUPIL'S PAGE HL10

Words and Music by
Kal Mann and Dave Appell
Piano Accompaniment by Mark Brymer

Down at the Twist and Shout

PUPIL'S PAGE HL12

Words and Music by Mary Chapin Carpenter
Piano Accompaniment by Mark Brymer

Twist and Shout

PUPIL'S PAGE HL14

Words and Music by
Bert Russell and Phil Medley
Piano Accompaniment by Mark Brymer

369

Land of a Thousand Dances

PUPIL'S PAGE HL16

Words and Music by Chris Kenner
Piano Accompaniment by Mark Brymer

Teacher's Notes

ACKNOWLEDGMENTS

Grateful acknowledgment is given to the following authors, composers, and publishers. Every effort has been made to trace the ownership of all copyrighted material and to secure the necessary permissions to reprint these selections. In the case of some selections for which acknowledgment is not given, extensive research has failed to locate the copyright holders.

Fran Smartt Addicott for *Let Music Surround You*.

Allyn and Bacon, Inc. for *The Wabash Cannonball* by William Kindt.

American Folklore Society for *Stone Pounding*, edited by T. Grame. Reprinted by permission of the American Folklore Society.

Irving Berlin for *It's a Lovely Day Today*.

Boosey & Hawkes, Inc. for *The Derby Ram* by Peter Erdei from 150 AMERICAN FOLK SONGS. Copyright © 1974 by Boosey & Hawkes, Inc. Reprinted by permission. For *Dormi, Dormi*, arranged by Mary Goetze. Copyright © 1984 by Boosey & Hawkes, Inc. This arrangement is made with the permission of Boosey & Hawkes, Inc. Reprinted by permission. *For The Path to the Moon* by Eric H. Thiman and Madeline C. Thomas. For *A Tragic Story* from FRIDAY AFTERNOONS by Benjamin Britten. © 1936 by Boosey & Co., Ltd.; Copyright renewed. Reprinted by permission of Boosey & Hawkes, Inc.

Margaret Campbelle-Holman for *And Where Is Home?* by Margaret Campbelle-Holman.

Canadian Museum of Civilization for *Feller from Fortune (Lots of Fish in Bonavist' Harbour)* from SONGS ON THE NEW-FOUNDLAND OUTPORTS by Kenneth Peacock. National Museum of Canada, Bulletin 197, Anthropological Series 65, vol. 1, Ottawa 1965.

Cherry Lane Music Publishing Company, Inc. for *Calypso* by John Denver. © 1975 Cherry Lane Music Publishing Company, Inc. This Arrangement © 1994 Cherry Lane Music Publishing Company, Inc. All Rights Reserved. Used By Permission. For *Garden Song* by David Mallet. © Copyright 1975 Cherry Lane Music Publishing Company, Inc. This Arrangement © Copyright 1994 Cherry Lane Music Publishing Company, Inc. for *Take Me Home, Country Roads*. Words and music by Bill Danoff, Taffy Nivert and John Denver.

Choristers Guild for *Come and Sing Together* from CANONS, SONGS AND BLESSINGS by Helen and John Kemp. Copyright © 1990 Choristers Guild. Used by permission.

Vernon Clark for *Martin's Cry* by Vernon Clark. © 1991 Vernon Clark.

CPP/Belwin, Inc. for *Donna Donna* by Sholom Secunda and Aaron Zeitlin. Copyright © 1940, 1950 (Renewed 1968) MILLS MUSIC INC., c/o EMI MUSIC PUBLISHING. World Print Rights Administered by CPP/BELWIN, INC. All Rights Reserved. For *Singin' in the Rain* by Nacio Herb Brown & Arthur Freed. Copyright © 1929 (Renewed 1957) METRO-GOLDWYN-MAYER, INC., Rights Assigned to ROBBINS MUSIC CORP. All Rights of ROBBINS MUSIC CORP. Assigned to EMI CATALOGUE PARTNERSHIP. All Rights Controlled and Administered by EMI ROBBINS CATALOG, INC. International Copyright Secured. Made in U.S.A. Used by Permission. For *Sir Duke* by Stevie Wonder. © 1976 by JOBETE MUSIC CO., INC., and BLACKBULL MUSIC, INC., Hollywood, CA. International Copyright Secured. Made in USA. All Rights Reserved.

Marilyn Davidson for the arrangement of *I Am a Cat*.

Dover Publications Inc. for *The California Song* from SONGS THE WHALEMEN SANG by Gale Huntington. © 1970 Dover Publications, Inc.

Fox Film Music Corporation for *Somewhere in My Memory* by John Williams and Leslie Bricusse.

Ganymede Music for THE GOLDEN GOOSE. © 1999 by Linda Worsley.

Hap-Pal Music for *The Eagle* by Hap Palmer and Martha Cheney. © 1976 Hap-Pal Music.

Harcourt Brace Jovanovich, Inc. for *Hi! Ho! The Rattlin' Bog* from HI! HO! THE RATTLIN' BOG AND OTHER FOLK SONGS FOR GROUP SINGING, copyright © 1969 by John Langstaff, reprinted by permission of Harcourt Brace Jovanovich, Inc.

The Heritage Music Press for *Don't Let the Music Stop* by Eugene Butler.

Neil A. Kjos Music Co. for *La Pájara Pinta* from CANTEMOS EN ESPANOL BOOK 1, © 1948, ren. 1975 Max and Beatrice Krone. Reprinted with permission 1992.

Rita Klinger for *Aquaqua del a Omar*, Israeli children's singing game, collected in Jerusalem, Israel, by Rita Klinger, 1980.

The Last Music Co. for *This Pretty Planet* by John Forster & Tom Chapin. © 1988 Limousine Music Co. & The Last Music Co. (ASCAP).

Limousine Music Co. for *This Pretty Planet* by John Forster & Tom Chapin. © 1988 Limousine Music Co. & The Last Music Co. (ASCAP).

McGraw-Hill Ryerson Ltd. for *The Old Carrion Crow*, a Nova Scotian folk song from TRADITIONAL SONGS FROM NOVA SCOTIA by Helen Creighton. © McGraw-Hill Ryerson Ltd.

Dale Marxen for *Waltzing with Bears* by Dale E. Marxen. © 1986 Dale Marxen.

MMB Music, Inc. for *The Cat Came Back* from THE CAT CAME BACK by Mary Goetze. © 1984 MMB Music, Inc., Saint Louis. Used by Permission. All Rights Reserved. For *Fed My Horse* from THE CAT CAME BACK by Mary Goetze. © 1984 MMB Music, Inc., Saint Louis. Used by Permission. All Rights Reserved.

For *Mongolian Night Song* from SONGS OF CHINA by Gloria Kiester and Martha Chrisman Riley. © 1988 MMB Music, Inc., Saint Louis. Used by Permission. All Rights Reserved.

Page Mortimer for the movement instructions for *Down the Road*.

Music Sales Corporation for *This Is My Country*. Words by Don Raye. Music by Al Jacobs. Copyright © 1940 (Renewed). Shawneed Press, Inc. and Warock Corp. International Copyright Secured. All Rights Reserved. Used By Permission. For *Winter Fantasy* by Jill Gallina. Copyright © 1982 Shawnee Press, Inc. International Copyright Secured. All Rights Reserved. Used by Permission.

José-Luis Orozco for *En la Feria de San Juan (aka La Feria de Atitlán/La Pulga de San José)*. © 1985 José-Luis Orozco. Music and Lyrics ARCOIRIS RECORDS, P.O. Box 7428, Berkeley, CA 94707.

Plymouth Music Co., Inc. for *Haida*. Arranged by Henry Leck.

Anthony Quinn Richardson for *I Can Be* by Anthony Q. Richardson. © 1991 by Anthony Quinn Richardson.

Roots & Branches Music, BMI for *Somos el barco (We Are the Boat)* by Lorre Wyatt.

St. Nicholas Music, Inc. for *A Holly Jolly Christmas*, Music and Lyrics by Johnny Marks. Copyright 1962, 1964 St. Nicholas Music, Inc., New York, New York, renewed 1990, 1992. All Rights Reserved. Used by Permission.

Scholastic, Inc. for *Boogie Woogie Ghost* by Nadine M. Peglar. Reprinted from INSTRUCTOR magazine, October 1973. Copyright © 1973 by Scholastic, Inc. Reprinted by permission of Scholastic, Inc.

Shawnee Press for *Sing a Song of Peace* by Jill Gallina.

Silver, Burdett & Ginn Inc. for *Michie Banjo*. English words by Margaret Marks, from MAKING MUSIC YOUR OWN © 1971 Silver Burdett Company. Used by permission. All rights reserved.

Kathy B. Sorensen for *Hoe Ana Te Vaka; San lun tsa; and Suk san wan pi mai*, collected and transcribed by Kathy Sorensen. © 1991 Kathy B. Sorensen.

Stratford Music Corp. for *Comes Once in a Lifetime* from SUBWAYS ARE FOR SLEEPING by Jule Styne (music), Betty Comden and Adolph Green (words).

Stormking Music, Inc. for *Song of the World's Last Whale* by Pete Seeger. © Copyright 1970, 1994 by STORMKING MUSIC INC. All Rights Reserved. Used by Permission.

Turnpike Tom Music for *City of New Orleans* by Steve Goodman.

Jerry Vogel Music Co., Inc. for *Macnamara's Band*. Unpub. American Version Copyright 1935 by Latham, Carlson & Bonham, renewed. Pub. American Version Copyright 1940 Jerry Vogel Music Co., Inc., renewed.

Warock Corporation for *This Is My Country*. Words by Don Raye. Music by Al Jacobs. Copyright © 1940 (Renewed). Shawnee Press, Inc. and Warock Corp. International Copyright Secured. All Rights Reserved. Used by Permission.

Word Music, Inc. for *Tree Song* by Ken Medema.

World Association of Girl Guides and Girl Scouts for *I Let Her Go, Go* from CANCIONES DE NUESTRA CABAÑA, copyright 1980 World Association of Girl Guides and Girl Scouts, reprinted by permission.

ACKNOWLEDGMENTS FOR HAL LEONARD SHOWSTOPPERS

Grateful acknowledgement is given to the following authors, composers, and publishers.

At the Hop Words and Music by Arthur Singer, John Madara and David White. Copyright © 1957 (Renewed) by Arc Music Corporation (BMI) and Six Continents Music Publishing, Inc. (BMI). All Rights Controlled by Arc Music Corporation (BMI). International Copyright Secured. All Rights Reserved. Used by Permission.

Bristol Stomp Words and Music by Kal Mann and Dave Appell. Copyright © 1961 Kalmann Music, Inc. Copyright Renewed. All Rights Controlled and Administered by Spirit Two Music, Inc. (ASCAP). International Copyright Secured. All Rights Reserved.

Dancing in the Street Words and Music by Marvin Gaye, Ivy Hunter and William Stevenson. © 1964 (Renewed 1992) FCG Music, NMG Music, MGIII Music, Jobete Music Co., Inc. and Stone Agate Music. All Rights Controlled and Administered by EMI April Music Inc. and EMI Blackwood Music Inc. on behalf of Jobete Music Co., Inc and Stone Agate Music (A Division of Jobete Music Co., Inc.). All Rights Reserved. International Copyright Secured. Used by Permission

Down At The Twist And Shout Words and Music by Mary Chapin Carpenter. © 1990 EMI April Music Inc. and Getarealjob Music. All Rights Controlled and Administered by EMI April Music Inc. All Rights Reserved. International Copyright Secured. Used by Permission

Land Of A Thousand Dances Words and Music by Chris Kenner. © 1963, 1970 (Renewed 1991) EMI Longitude Music. All Rights Reserved. International Copyright Secured. Used by Permission

The Loco-Motion Words and Music by Gerry Goffin and Carole King. © 1962 (Renewed 1990) Screen Gems-EMI Music Inc. All Rights Reserved. International Copyright Secured. Used by Permission.

Twist and Shout Words and Music by Bert Russell and Phil Medley. Copyright © 1960, 1964 Sony/ATV Songs LLC, Unichappell Music Inc. and Sloopy II Music. Copyright Renewed All Rights on behalf of Sony/ATV Songs LLC Administered by Sony/ATV Music Publishing, 8 Music Square West, Nashville, TN 37203. International Copyright Secured. All Rights Reserved

We Got the Beat Words and Music by Charlotte Caffey. Copyright © 1981 by BMG Songs, Inc. International Copyright Secured. All Rights Reserved.

Alphabetical Song Index

A
Ah, Poor Bird 285
Alleluia, Amen 281
Alouette 292
America 182
America, the Beautiful 178
And Where Is Home? 302
Aquaqua 132
Artsa Alinu (Our Land) 288
At the Hop 388

B
Babylon's Fallin' 250
Barter Song 326
Before Dinner 272
Bird in the Water 330
Boll Weevil, The 278
Bonhomme! Bonhomme! 194
Boogie Woogie Ghost, The 183
Bristol Stomp 358

C
California Song, The 38
Calypso 125
Cat Came Back, The 158
Chickalileeo 286
City of New Orleans 41
Come and Sing Together 84
Comes Once in a Lifetime 146
Court of King Carraticus, The ..164

D
Dancing in the Street 343
Dale, dale, dale! 209
Derby Ram, The 263
Dinah 254
Don't Let the Music Stop 307
Don't Let the Music Stop 2
Donna, Donna 172
Dormi, dormi (Sleep, Sleep) ...217
Down at the Twist and Shout ..364
Down by the Riverside 234
Down the Road 57
Dry Bones 188

E
Eagle, The 87
En la feria de San Juan
  (In the Market of San Juan) ..55
Entren santos peregrinos
  (Enter, Holy Pilgrims) 208

F
Fed My Horse 37
For Health and Strength 192
Four White Horses 50

G
Garden Song 170
Ghost of John, The 187
Go 'Round the Mountain 249

H
Haida 300
Hambone 118
Happiness 310
Heave-Ho Me Laddies 260
Hei Tama Tu Tama 131
Hi! Ho! The Rattlin' Bog 35
Hoe Ana Te Vaka
  (Paddle the Canoe) 110
Holly Jolly Christmas, A 211
Hop Up and Jump Up 273
Hosanna, Me Build a House ..103

I
I Am a Cat 252
I Can Be 149
I Don't Care If the Rain
  Comes Down 74
I Let Her Go, Go 27
I Love the Mountains 246
I's the B'y 90
Ida Red 255
In the Window 202
It's a Lovely Day Today 96

J
John Kanaka 283

K
Korobushka 289

L
La pájara pinta
  (The Speckled Bird) 76
Lady, Come Down and See ..253
Las mañanitas
  (The Morning Song) 143
Land of a Thousand Dances ..374
Let Music Surround You 9
Little David, Play on Your Harp .109
Loco-Motion, The 353
Lots o' Fish in Bonavist' Harbor .266

M
Macnamara's Band 238
Martin's Cry 230
Michie Banjo 166
Mince Pie or Pudding, A 193
Mongolian Night Song 32
Music Alone Shall Live
  (Himmel und Erde) 136
My Dame Hath a Lame,
  Tame Crane 270
My Horses Ain't Hungry 262

N
Night Song 248
No Matter What 317

O
O musique 291
O Tannenbaum!
  (O, Christmas Tree!) 214
Oh, Susanna 72
Oh, Won't You Sit Down? 7
Old Carrion Crow, The 52
Old Chisholm Trail, The 257
Old Dan Tucker 268
Old Joe Clark 162
Old Tar River 258
Oliver Cromwell 275
One More River 81
Orchestra Song 67
Over the Sea to Skye 94

P
Page's Train 251
Para pedir posada 204
Path to the Moon, The 293
Pay Me My Money Down 79
Push the Business On 144

S
San lun tsa (Three-Wheeled
  Taxi) 282
Sarasponda 108
Simple Gifts 168
Sing a Song of Peace 180
Singin' in the Rain 70
Sir Duke 18
Somewhere in My Memory 215
Somos el barco (We Are the Boat) 10
Song of the World's Last
  Whale, The 120
Sourwood Mountain 114
Star-Spangled Banner, The ...175
Stone Pounding 101
Suk san wan pi mai
  (New Year's Song) 228
Swapping Song 60

T
Take Me Home, Country Roads ..22
Take Time in Life 123
Things That Grow 322
This Is My Country 16
This Pretty Planet 156
Tina Singu 100
To Stop the Train 271
Tragic Story, A 116
Trail to Mexico 48
Tree Song 242
Tum-Balalaika 129
Twelve Days of Christmas, The .222
Twist and Shout 369

W
Wabash Cannonball, The 14
'Way Down Yonder in the Brickyard. 29
Wade in the Water 133
Waltzing with Bears 138
We Got the Beat 348
We Three Kings 220
When I First Came to This Land ..92
When I Was a Lad 62
Who's Got a Fishpole? 277
Wind on the Hill 298
Winter Fantasy 197